DIGITAL PHOTOGRAPHY BASICS

Nicki Toizer

2017

ISBN: 978-0-9991412-0-5 (paperback)
ISBN: 978-0-9991412-1-2 (e-book)

Library of Congress Control Number: 2017911160

Toizer Publishing
Glenside, PA
www.Toizer.com

Acknowledgements

I am indebted to those who have passed on some tidbit of photography wisdom to me over the years, including those who inspired me to pick up a camera in the first place: my dad, Alfred Toizer, and my grandfather, Bernard Rosenberg. Their encouragement to keep taking pictures, even when the results were not what I wanted, helped me to learn how to do it better the next time.

Thank you to those who served as models in some examples: Kelly Hoffman and Shiloh Bloom. Further gratitude to friends and family who took the time to proofread the book and provided suggestions for improvement.

Contents

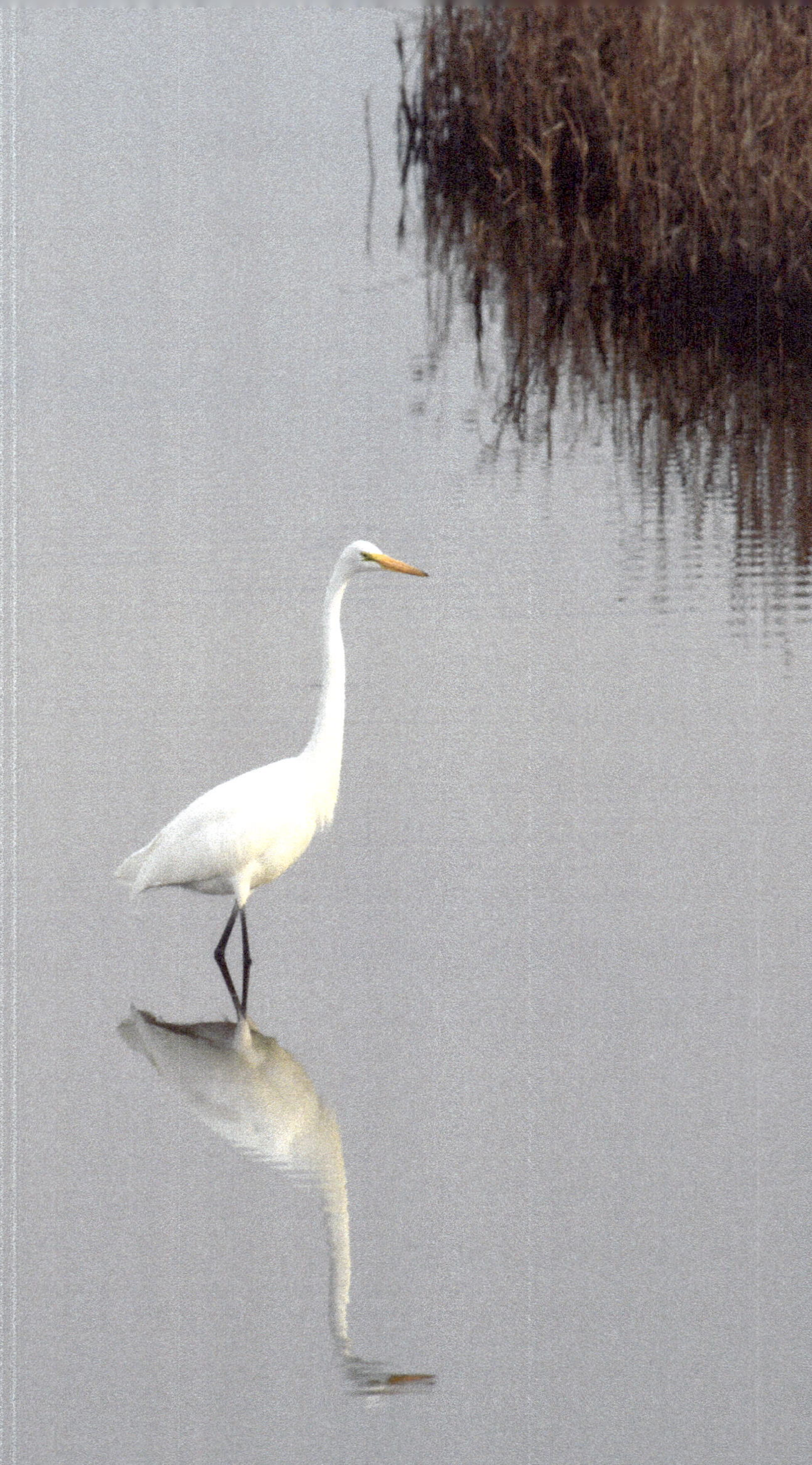

Great Egret. Nikon D3200, shutter priority, matrix metering, 1/400 sec, f/11, ISO 400, 450 mm. Assateague Island, VA.

Introduction

If you enjoy photography and want to take better pictures but you're stuck on Auto... welcome! Perhaps you know a little about shutter speed and aperture but you're not sure how to take advantage of them. You're in the right place!

I have geared the information here toward novices and those who would like more information before taking their camera off Auto. This will be most useful for those who have an advanced point-and-shoot (sometimes called a bridge camera), digital SLRs, and mirrorless cameras (see page 5) where you have control over exposure settings. Look for a dial on the top with the following letters: P, S, A, & M or P, Tv, Av, & M. There may be other symbols on that dial, too, but these letters are the important ones that will give you the creative controls described within.

This is not a camera manual. There are too many different models in use and more on the way to be able to provide that level of individual detail. You may need to consult your camera's manual to learn how to make the various adjustments discussed in the following pages.

Topics covered here are meant to supplement your manual by giving greater detail on the results you can achieve by changing your settings. Other chapters cover what I wish I knew early on in my photography hobby – things like aspect ratio and what that means when you want to make larger prints.

The chapters are organized for those new to photography so if you are already comfortable with the early information, feel free to skip ahead to the parts you're eager to learn.

Ready? Let's go.

ASIDE: You will notice the exposure details for most images included in this book. They include the camera used, what mode I was using (such as shutter priority, aperture priority, or manual), metering mode, shutter speed, aperture, ISO, focal length of the lens, the exposure compensation (if used), and the location.

RIGHT: Cowboy with camera. Minolta Maxxum 7D, shutter priority, spot metering, 1/1000 sec, f/8, ISO 400, 300 mm, -0.7 EV. Craig, CO.

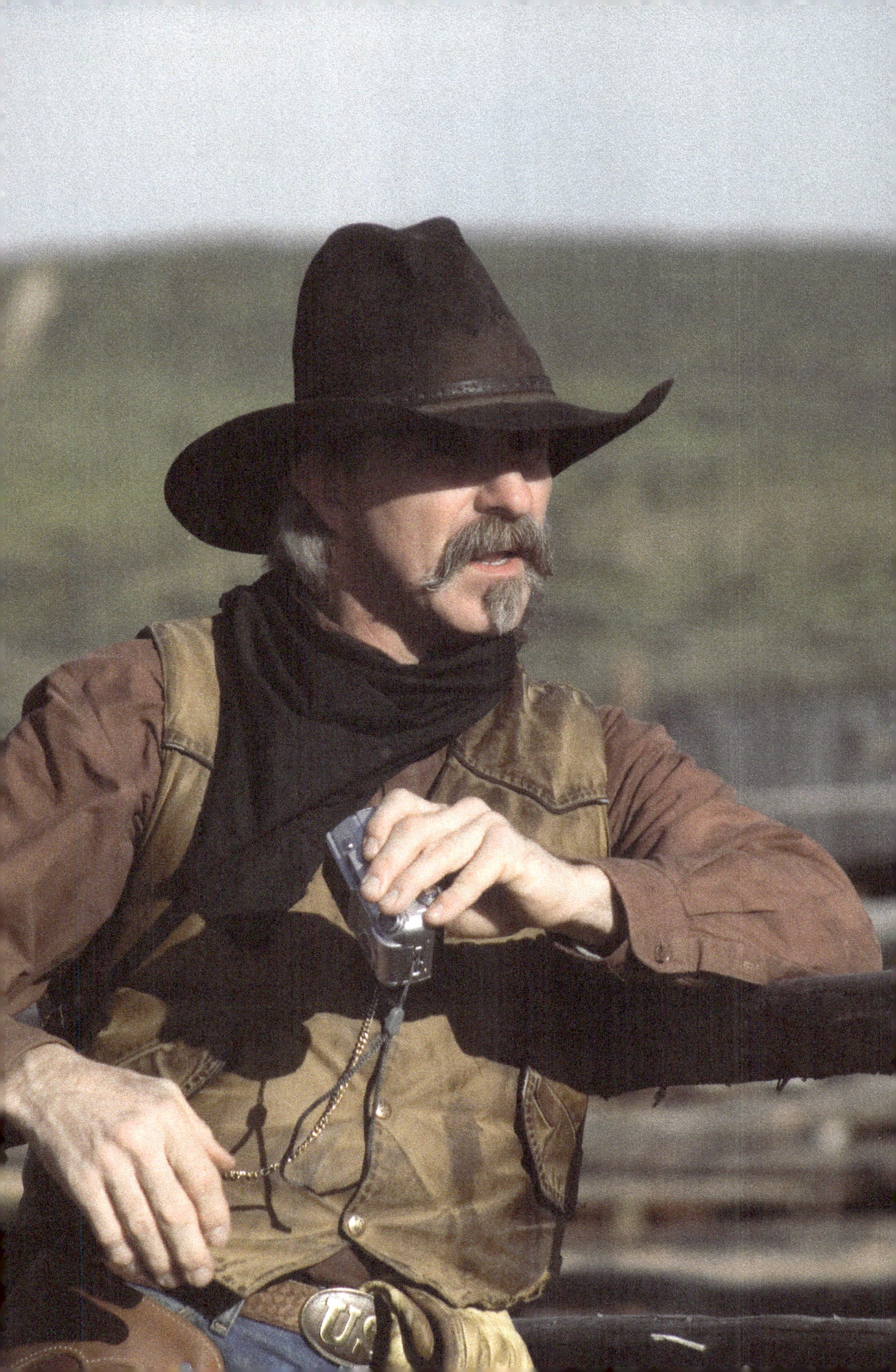

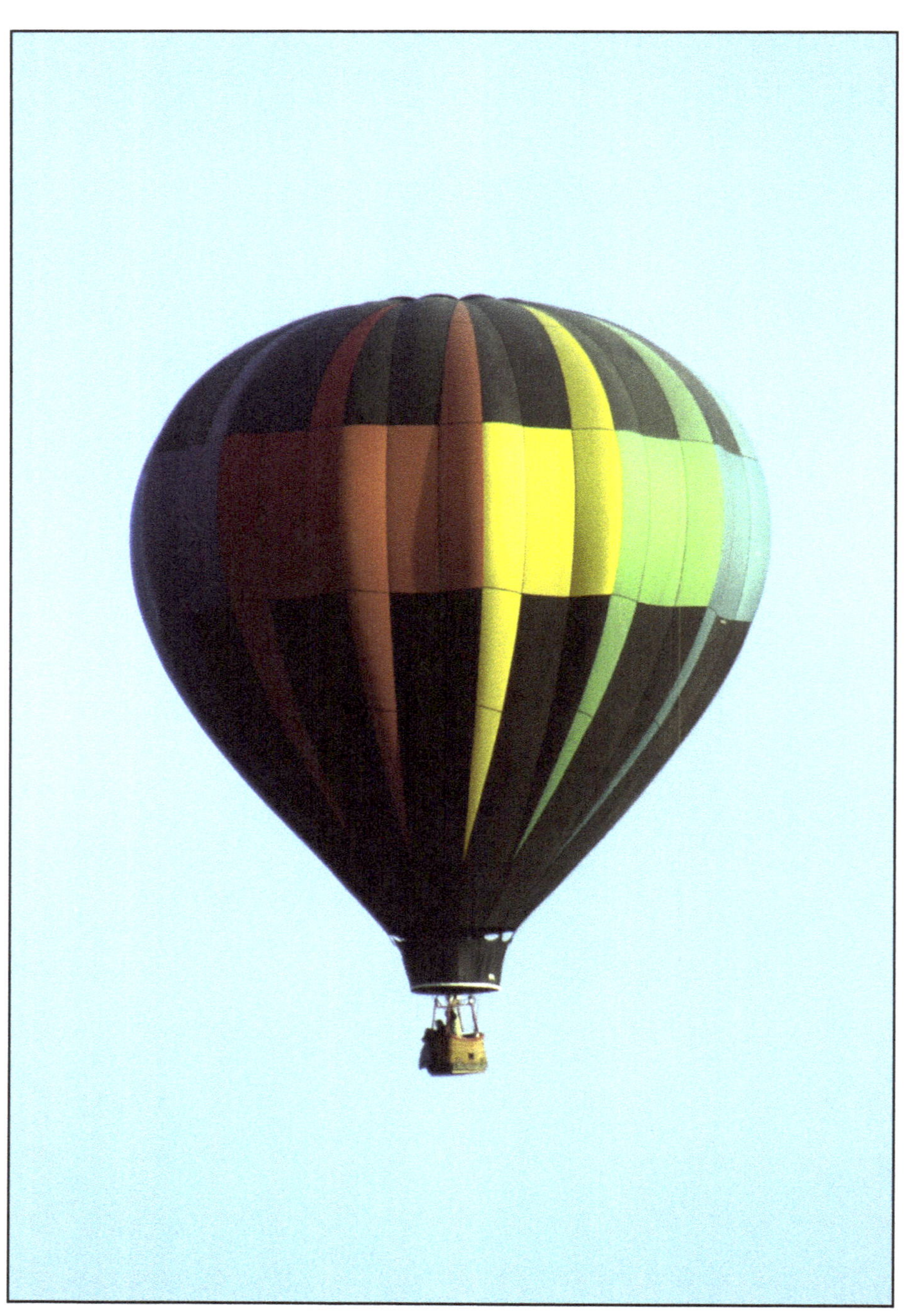

Minolta Maxxum 7D, shutter priority, pattern metering, 1/200 sec, f/8, ISO 100, 450 mm. Tucson, AZ.

1.

The Lingo

Camera Types

Point-and-Shoot cameras are meant to be very simple to use and provide the photographer with just a few settings they can change. They range in size from very small (fit in your chest pocket) to medium-sized (can be stashed in your purse or small bag; might have a grip for your right hand to hold).

DSLR stands for digital single lens reflex. When you look through the viewfinder, a mirror and prism allow you to actually see through the lens and accurately compose the image. Pushing the shutter button down all the way to take the picture flips the mirror out of the way to capture the image on the sensor. The photographer has access to change many settings as well as use a variety of different lenses.

Bridge cameras are generally larger versions of point-and-shoots that provide more settings to change (such as shutter and aperture) but not the lens. They typically have a viewfinder and are shaped more like an SLR.

Mirrorless cameras have all the setting controls of an SLR without the mirror that needs to move out of the way when you

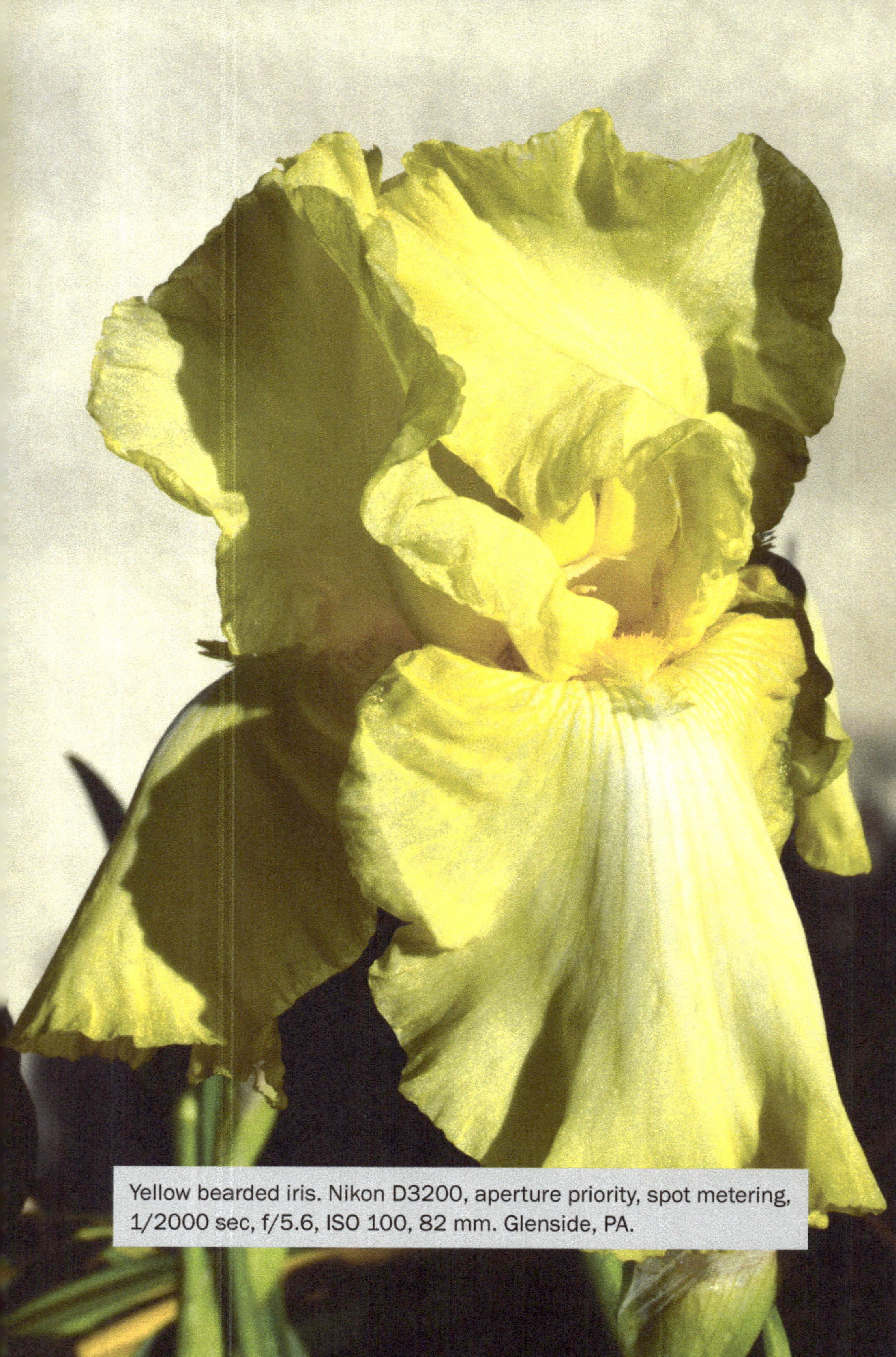

Yellow bearded iris. Nikon D3200, aperture priority, spot metering, 1/2000 sec, f/5.6, ISO 100, 82 mm. Glenside, PA.

press the shutter button. They also have interchangeable lenses.

You will get the most out of this book if you have a bridge, DSLR, or mirrorless camera. However, bridge cameras tend to limit the range of shutter speeds and/or apertures you can choose so you will not have the same amount of control over exposure.

Pixel

What is it? A pixel (short for picture element) is the building block of your digital image. It's the tiny blocks of color that make up your photo. The more pixels, the more detail gets recorded, and the larger you can print (or the more you can crop). A megapixel is one million pixels, abbreviated 1 MP.

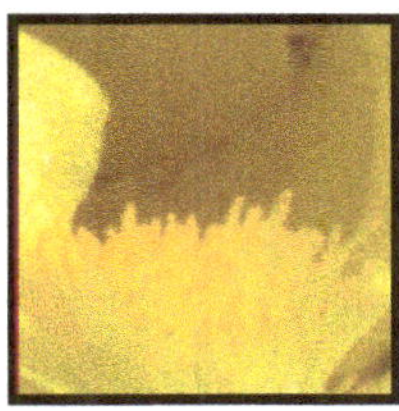

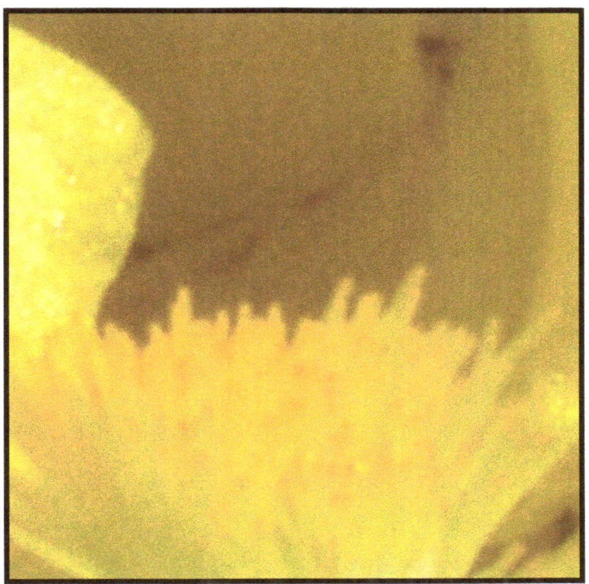

Above is a 1" x 1" section of the iris to the left, shot at 6 MP (2000 x 3008 pixels). To the right is that section enlarged 3x. You can start to see some of the blocky "pixelation."

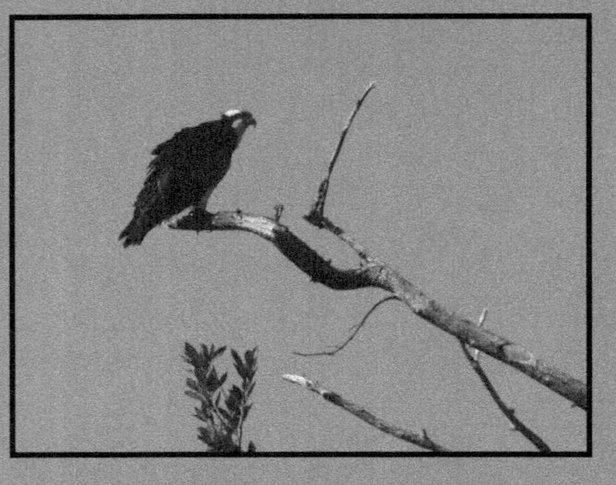

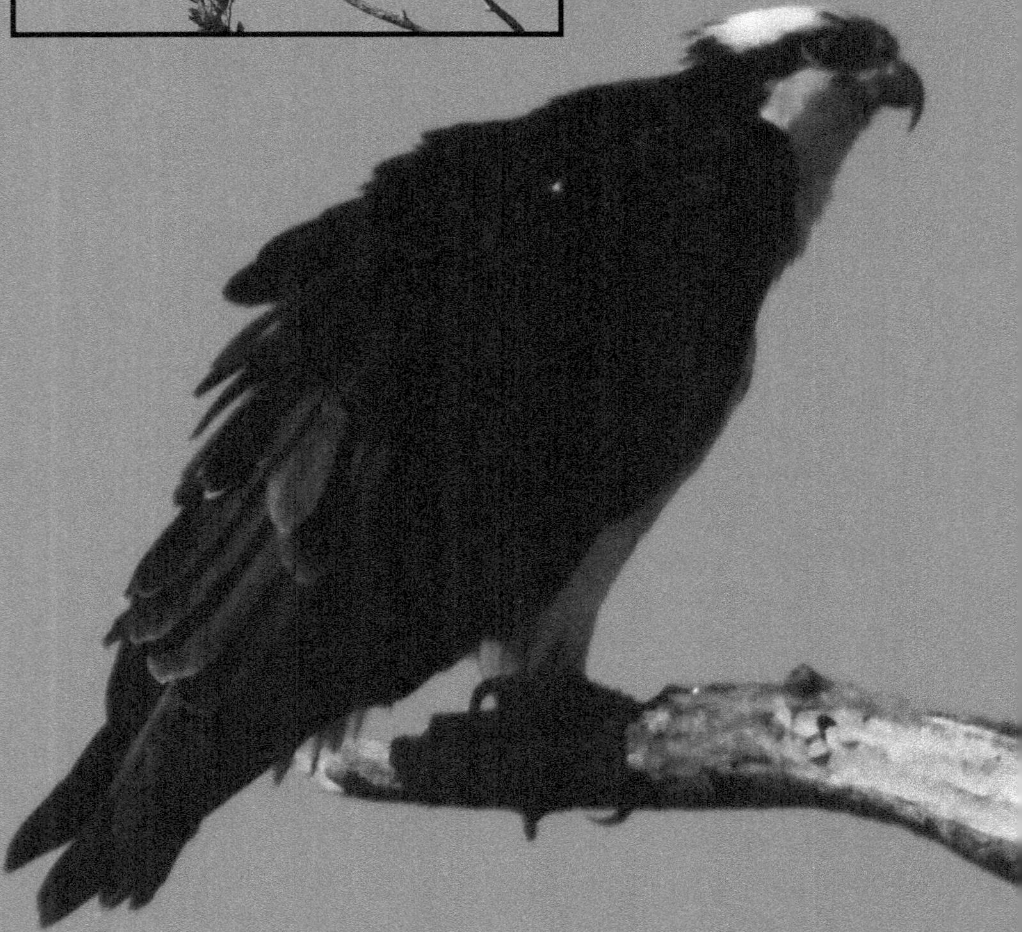

Osprey. Sony A700, shutter priority, center-weighted metering, 1/640 sec, f/13, ISO 200, 450 mm. "Ding" Darling National Wildlife Refuge, Sanibel, FL.

What you are most likely to notice is that a small 4" x 6" print will look sharper than a cropped enlargement. See the example to the left. The 4" x 6" looks great. But when the image gets cropped and enlarged so that the osprey is nice and big, now it starts to look blurry, especially around the edges.

Why you might care: If you want to print large sizes (11" x 14" and up), you'll want more pixels.

Aspect Ratio

What is it? Aspect ratio is the width:height of your image expressed as the smallest whole number possible, such as 3:2 (rather than 6:4) to represent a standard 4" x 6" print.

Why you might care: Traditional photography has an aspect ratio of 3:2, meaning that a 4" x 6" print is the full frame. This is what most of us are used to getting when we make prints. Your camera, especially point-and-shoot models may offer you the option of 4:3 (similar to older TVs and computer monitors) or 16:9 (wide-screen). If you choose 4:3, you'll lose some of your image when you print 4" x 6". Wide-screen has potential for panoramic prints (long, skinny prints that will require custom framing). Printing 16:9 images in traditional sizes will lose a lot more of the image (see page 13).

Aspect ratio is most important when making enlargements. For example, 8" x 10" loses two inches of image from a full-frame 8" x 12" print (i.e., an aspect ratio of 3:2). If you want to fit the full image on an 8" x 10" print, you will have white borders on the long sides.

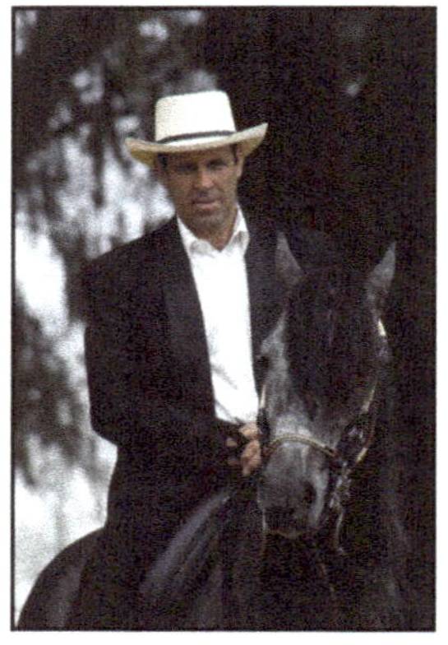 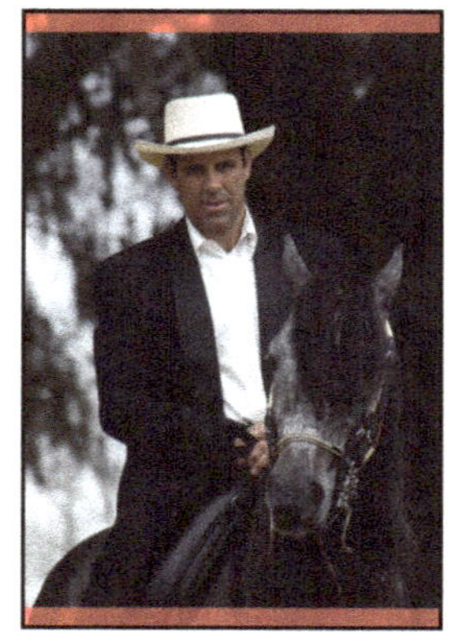 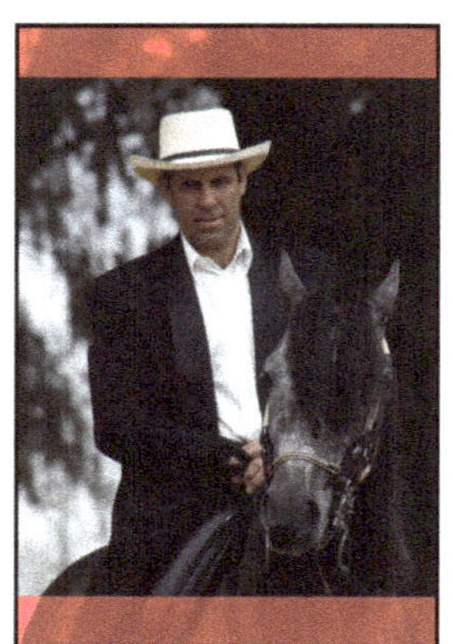

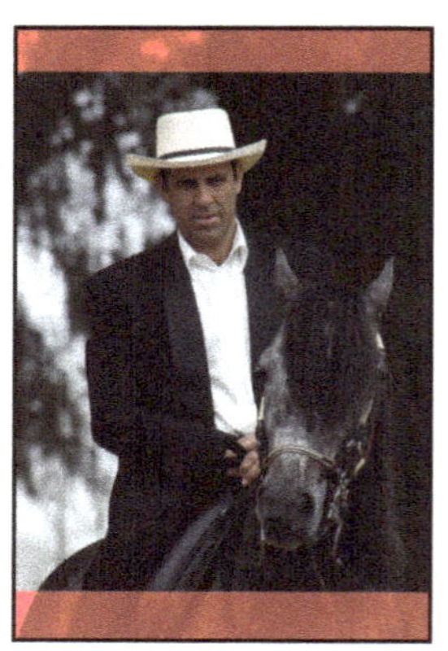

Clockwise from top left: 4" x 6" full frame; 5" x 7" enlargement; 8" x 10" enlargement; 11" x 14" enlargement. Areas in red show what gets cropped automatically when enlarged.

Horse & Rider. Minolta Maxxum 7D, shutter priority, pattern metering, 1/300 sec, f/9, ISO 400, 450 mm. Ocala, FL.

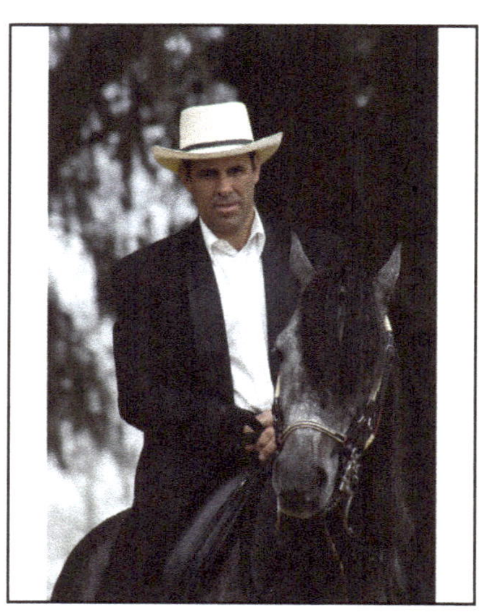

Full frame fitted onto an 8" x 10" print so nothing gets cropped but now there are white borders on the sides. This would need a custom mat for framing.

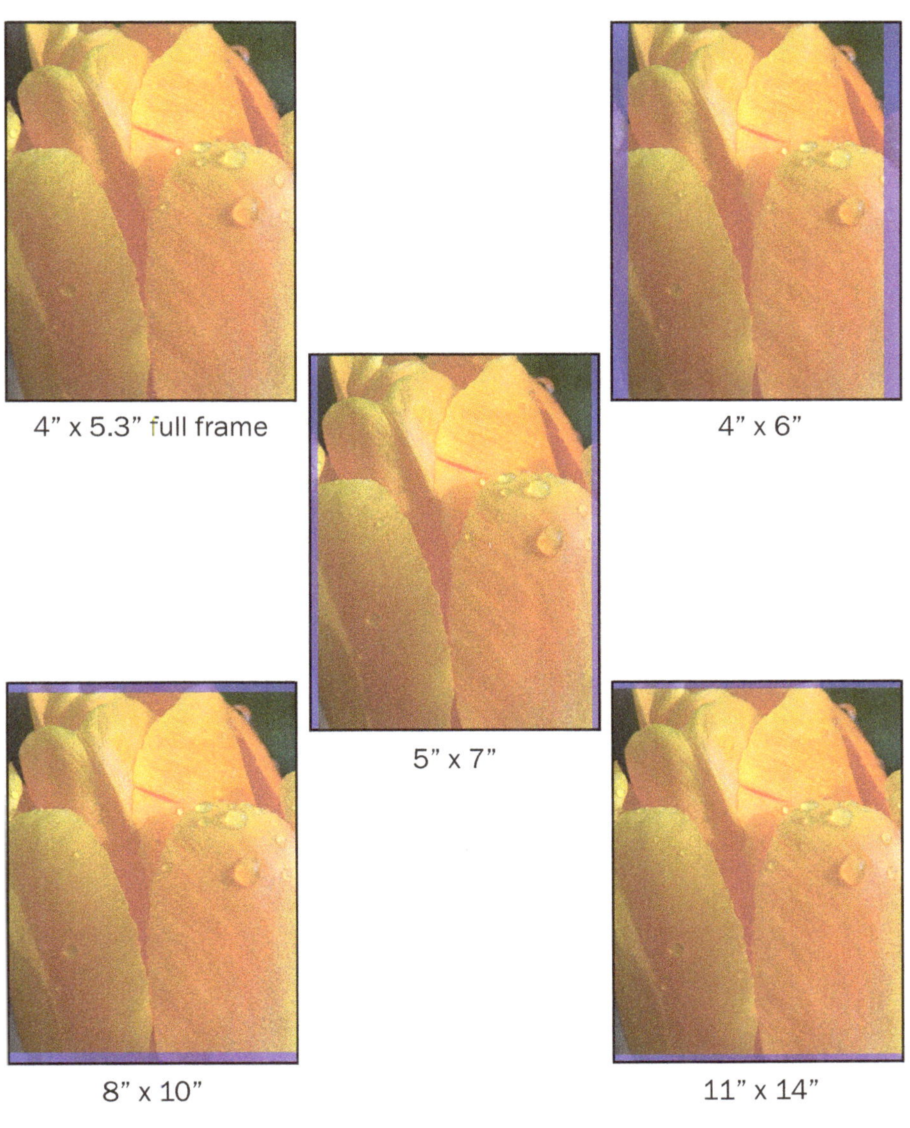

Tulip. Sony CD1000, auto, center-weighted metering, 1/370 sec, f/4, ISO 80, 28 mm. Awbury Arboretum, Philadelphia, PA.

Areas in purple show what gets cropped automatically when enlarged.

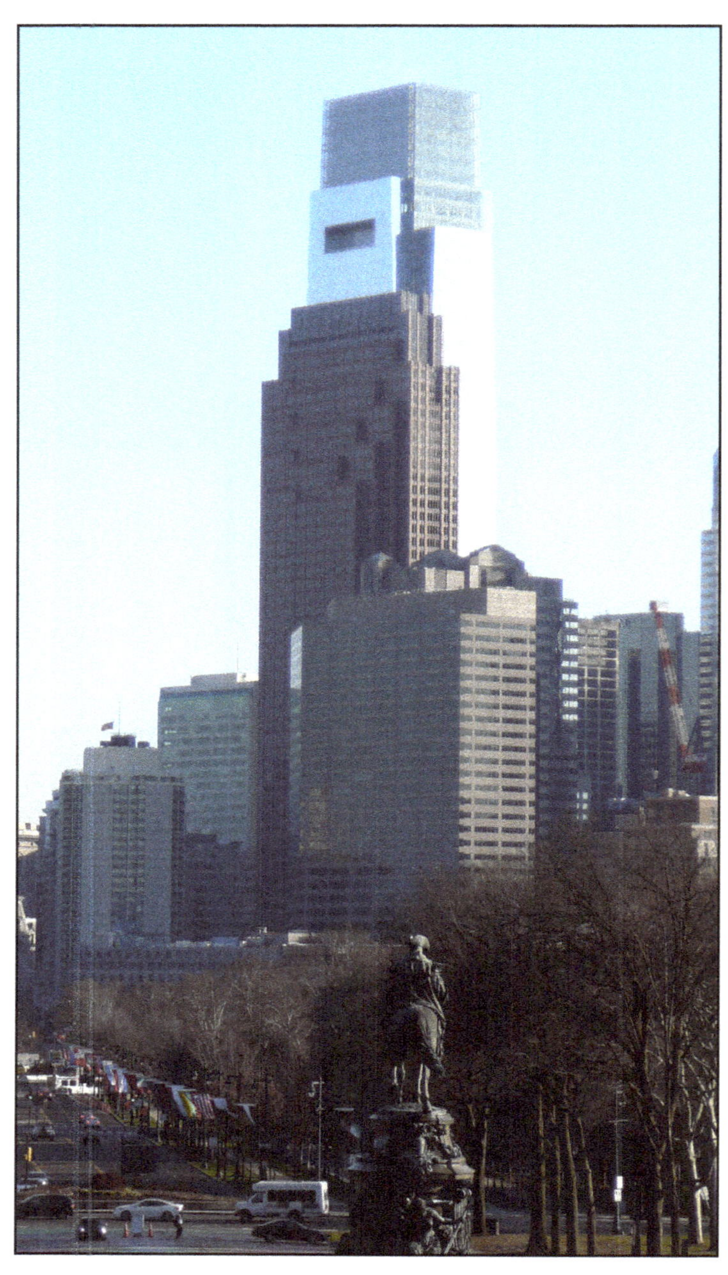

Full frame, 16:9 wide-screen image.
Center City Philadelphia with Comcast Tower. Panasonic DMC-TZ1, auto, pattern metering, 1/800 sec, f/4.0, ISO 100, 149 mm.

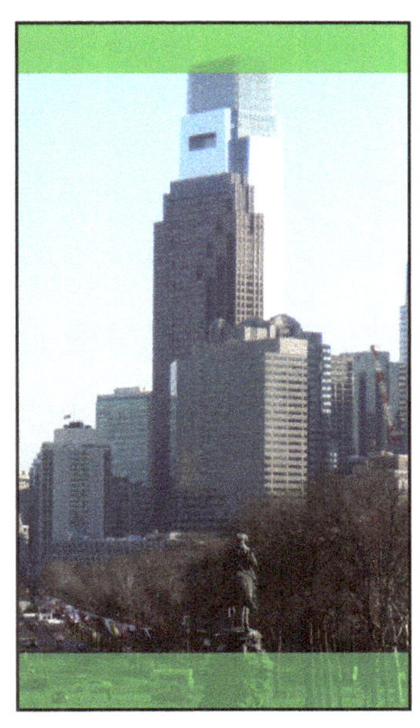
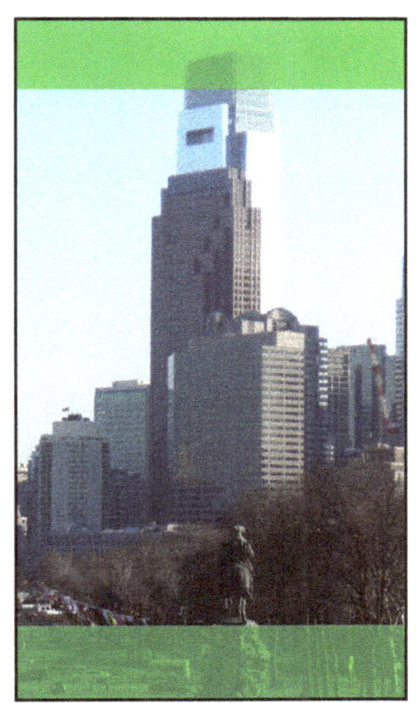
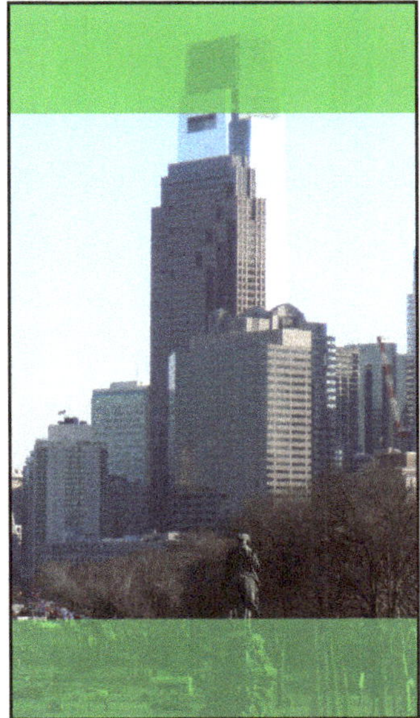

Clockwise from top left: 16:9 wide-screen printed as a 4" x 6" print, 5" x 7" enlargement, and 8" x 10" enlargement. Areas in green show what gets cropped automatically when printed.

File Types

What's the difference between JPG and RAW? Plenty!

.JPG (or JPEG) is universal – every computer should be able to open up a JPG without any fuss. The camera processes the photo, using various algorithms and internal settings. It's a compressed file format and is affected by quality settings such as Extra Fine, Fine, Normal, and Basic. Extra Fine (if available) is the least compressed and therefore the largest file size with the most information. Basic is the most compressed, smallest file size, and lowest quality.

RAW saves all the information needed to process and reprocess your photo. Its file size can be 2-4x the size of a .jpg file. Each manufacturer uses their own proprietary format and 3-letter extension (such as .NEF for Nikon, .CR2 for Canon, .ARF for Sony, etc.). A separate computer program is required to process and view the image. Professional photographers use this format to ensure more usable images because they can essentially re-develop their images, if necessary.

If your camera can shoot in RAW, you received a CD/DVD with a program from the manufacturer to view/process the files. You can also purchase software. You'll need to install it before you can view any RAW images on your computer. Don't use this format unless you want to spend additional hours at the computer, processing all the images from your latest shoot before you can share or print them.

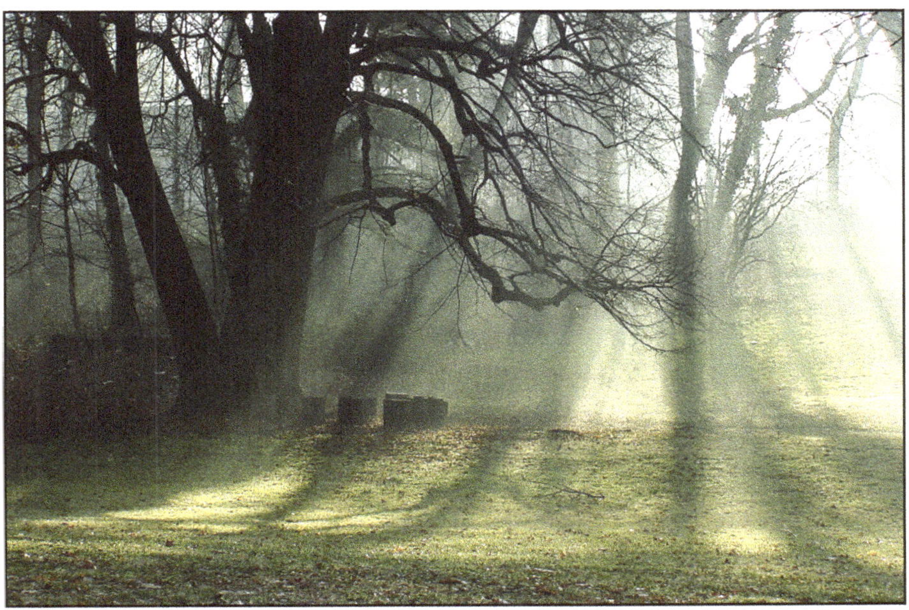

Woodland Halo. Sony CD1000, auto, center-weighted average, 1/135 sec, f/4, ISO 80, 17 mm. Awbury Arboretum, Philadelphia, PA.

2.
Lens Basics

Focal Length

The lens takes in light and focuses it onto the sensor so the camera can create an image. Focal length is the distance, in millimeters (mm), from your lens to the sensor. A wide angle lens (such as 10 mm up to about 28 mm), takes in a wide view of the world and may distort that view (such as a fisheye lens). A "normal" lens, usually 35 mm and up to 55 mm, takes in the view similar to your own field of view (without the peripheral vision). Telephoto lenses (70 mm and larger) bring far away subjects much closer. See the examples to the right.

The focal length is what you're referring to when you say you have a 28-55 mm, 70-200 mm, 90 mm, or 300 mm lens. Lenses with a range are commonly called zoom lenses.

Complicating this discussion are the cameras with smaller sensor sizes. Some cameras are full frame, most are smaller. If the sensor is smaller than a 35 mm negative, those cameras typically have a magnification factor of 1.3x-1.6x, depending on the camera. Multiply that factor by the focal length to get the equivalent 35 mm focal length for your camera. So an 18 mm lens on a camera with a 1.5x magnification factor is the equivalent of a 27 mm lens.

$$18 \text{ mm} \times 1.5 = 27 \text{ mm}$$

And a 300 mm lens becomes 450 mm. This is wonderful for those who like using a telephoto lens, but a challenge for those looking to shoot at really wide angles.

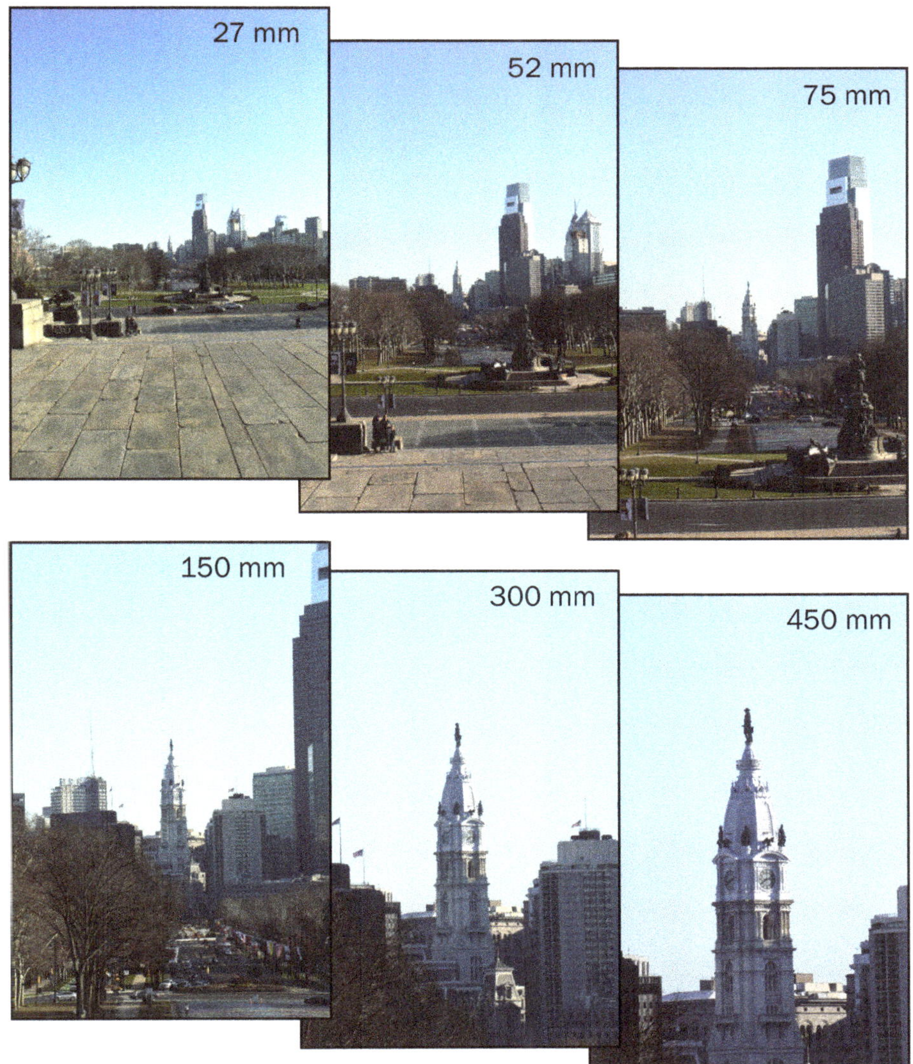

Aperture/ f-stop

The aperture is the opening within the lens that allows light
to enter your camera and create an image on the sensor. Your
aperture range is **dependent on the lens**, not your camera,
and so will vary from lens to lens. A so-called "fast" lens has a
very wide maximum aperture, such as f/1.4 or f/2.8, allowing
you to use faster shutter speeds. Lenses with larger openings
are more expensive since they use better optics than lenses
that have smaller maximum apertures. Many zoom lenses have
different maximum apertures at different focal lengths (i.e.,
f/4.5 at 55 mm and f/5.6 at 300 mm). Higher-end zoom lenses
(more expensive) can maintain a large aperture (such as f/2.8)
throughout the entire zoom range.

Filter Size

The filter size refers to the diameter of the glass at the front
of the lens. This is denoted somewhere on the lens with this
symbol: ø followed by a number, such as ø55. Learn more about
filters starting on page 89.

3.

Getting Started

Diopter

If you have a DSLR, it likely has a small dial close to the viewfinder that acts like eyeglasses. Turn on your camera and press the shutter button down halfway to focus on something. Keep it pointed at that subject and rotate the diopter with your thumb or finger to see the difference. Once you find the position where the scene is most in focus, leave it there. Due to its location on the camera, you are unlikely to move it later by accident.

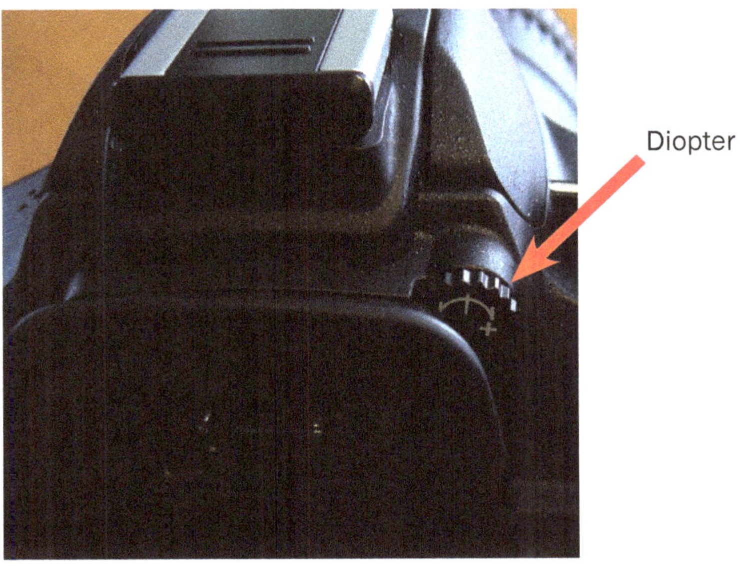

Image Size and Quality

Your camera gives you a few options such as large, medium, and small. Large has the most pixels and your camera may show you exactly how many pixels are involved or it may indicate the number of megapixels for each size (such as 6 MP, 12 MP, or 24 MP). If you plan to make prints, especially larger than 8" x 10", choose more pixels. If you anticipate only sharing on social media or printing no larger than 5" x 7", you can choose a smaller size.

There's some trade off here. Larger pixel dimensions make larger files, so fewer images will fit on your media card than if you choose smaller pixel dimensions. This was more of a problem when media cards had smaller capacities (less than 2 GB). If you choose to shoot at larger pixel dimensions, be sure to use media cards with a larger capacity to accommodate more images, especially if you're travelling.

In digital photography, "quality" refers to the amount of compression the camera applies when saving the image as a JPG (this makes the file size smaller, but throws away information). I'm not a big fan of "Normal," so I choose "Fine" or "Extra Fine," if available. These settings throw away the least amount of information and result in larger file sizes.

Canon typically combines image size and quality. Look for these icons in the menu:

◢L ◢▮L ◢M ◢▮M ◢S ◢▮S

The L, M, and S indicate image size (Large, Medium, and Small) while the smooth arc is high quality and the stair-step indicates lower quality.

You may want to set check your image size and quality now to make sure they meet your needs. Consult your manual for directions on how to change these settings.

Holding the Camera Correctly

Keeping your camera steady while photographing will yield sharp photos. If you're hand-holding the camera (rather than using a monopod or tripod), you'll get the best results by using the viewfinder rather than composing through the LCD screen.

Most cameras have a right-handed grip and you'll find that the controls you'll need most often are within easy reach of your index finger on the top and your thumb on the back of the camera. Put your left hand, palm up, under the camera body and/ or the lens. If you're using a DSLR or mirrorless with a zoom lens, you'll easily be able to zoom the lens in and out or focus manually, if desired, with your left hand.

Bring your elbows in close to your body and stand with your

feet about shoulder-width apart. You can also take advantage of walls or trees to lean against for further support.

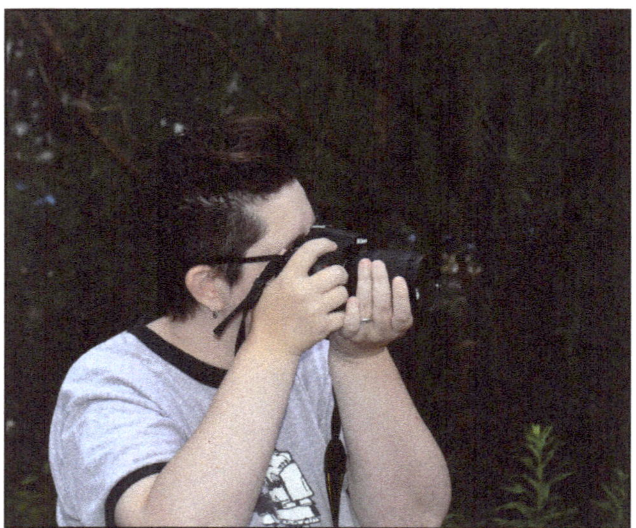

Proper camera technique for a horizontal image.

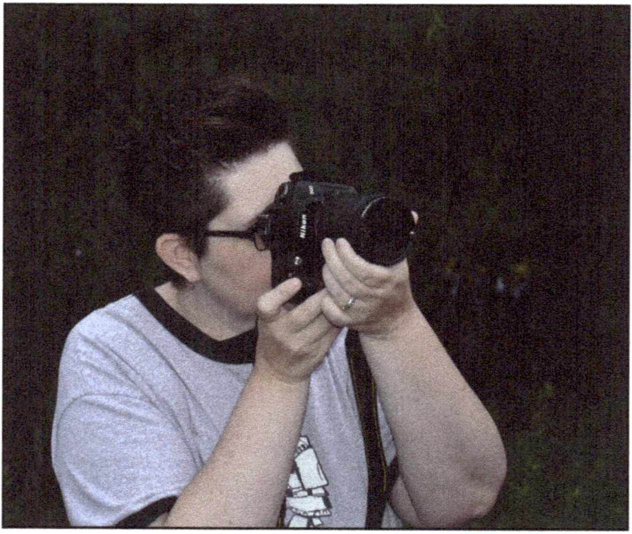

Proper camera technique for a vertical image.

4.

Exposure

Photography is all about light and how much (or how little) your camera needs to make a good image. The camera has two ways of physically controlling the amount of light entering the camera: the speed of the shutter (how fast it opens/closes) and the aperture (how wide the lens opens). If the scene you're photographing is dark, you will need the shutter open for longer and/or the aperture open wider than if you're shooting under bright conditions.

You will often hear the term "stop" in photography – it refers to exposure values and the doubling or halving the amount of light you're letting in to take the photo. It's a convenient way to compare exposures as shutter, aperture, and ISO all use different units. A full stop is expressed as 1 EV and can be either positive or negative, depending on whether you are making the image brighter (+) or darker (-). Your camera may allow adjustments in 1/3 or 1/2 stops.

Let's cover the individual parts of exposure: shutter duration, aperture, and ISO.

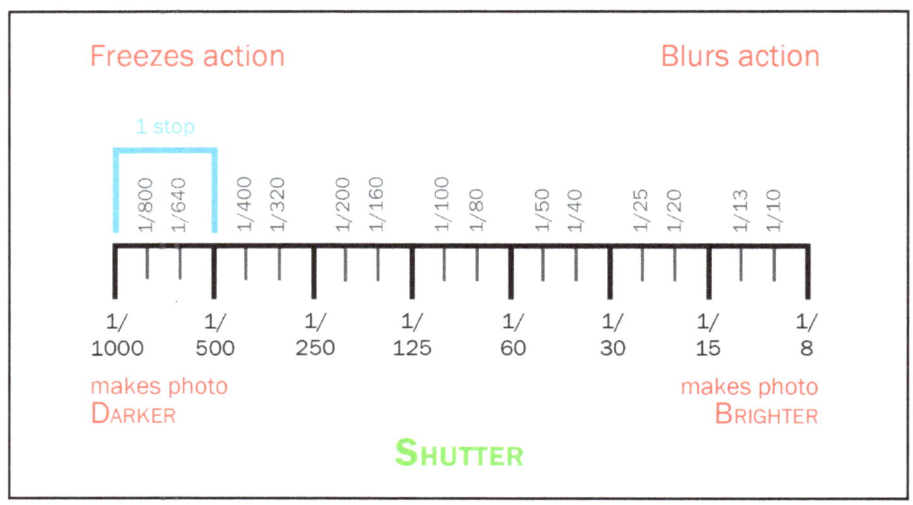

Table 4.1 Shutter duration.

Shutter Duration

This is the length of time the shutter is open to let light into the camera and make an exposure. On the next page is a chart of possible shutter durations (often referred to as shutter speed), in fractions of a second, you can choose. Those in bold are typical speeds available since the film era. They are one stop of exposure from the previous/next one in bold and have a half/ double relationship (1/30 is twice as fast as 1/15 but half as fast as 1/60). Your camera may or may not have all the options listed.

Using slow shutter durations will show more motion blur and may be difficult to hold the camera still without a tripod (1/30 second and below, typically). Using a faster shutter speed will freeze the action and reduce the possibility of camera shake.

1" (1 second, slow)	1/1.6	**1/2**
1/2.5	1/3	**1/4**
1/5	1/6	**1/8**
1/10	1/13	**1/15**
1/20	1/25	**1/30**
1/40	1/50	**1/60**
1/80	1/100	**1/125**
1/160	1/200	**1/250**
1/320	1/400	**1/500** (fast)
1/640	1/800	**1/1000**
1/1250	1/1600	**1/2000**
1/2500	1/3200	**1/4000** (very fast)

Table 4.2. Shutter speeds in seconds (slow-fast), from left to right.

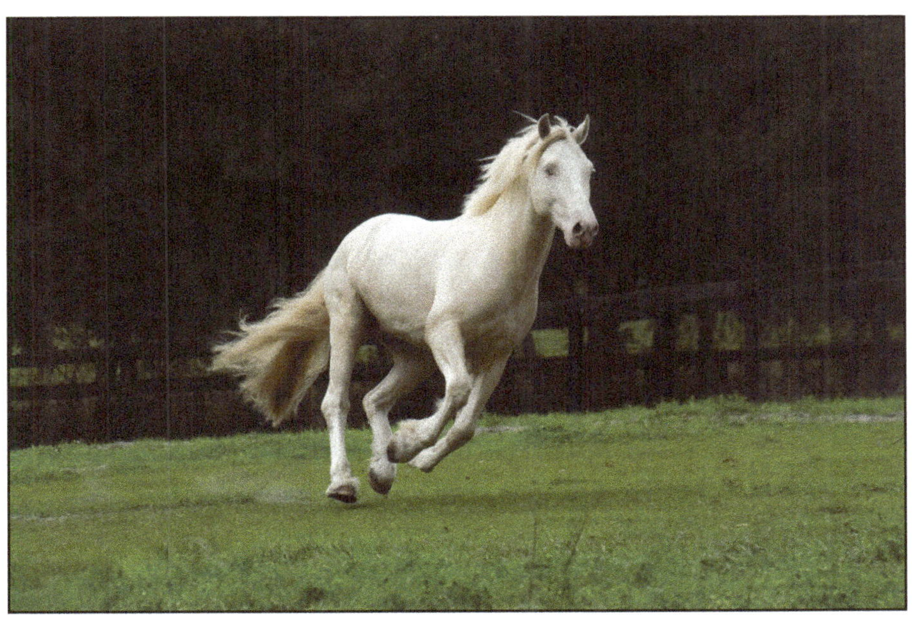

Minolta Maxxum 7D, shutter priority, pattern metering, 1/500 sec, f/5.6, ISO 400, 240 mm. Ocala, FL.

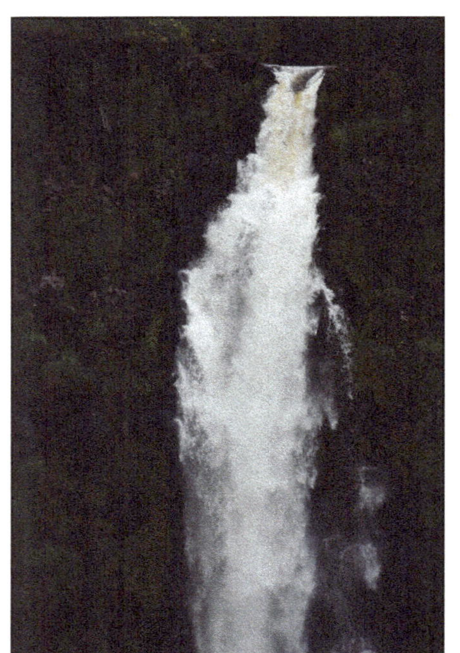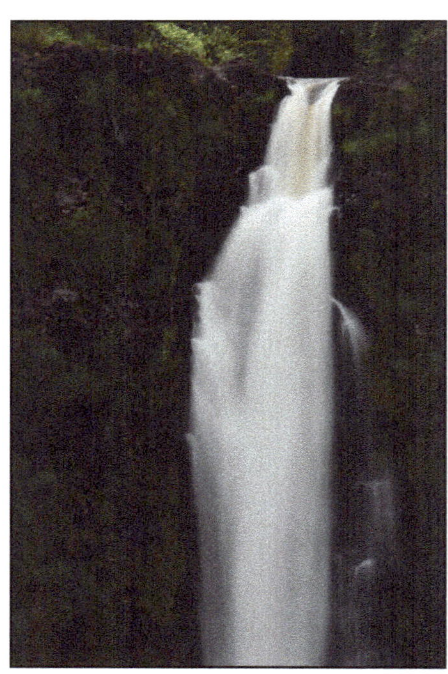

Nikon D7000, manual, pattern metering, ISO 160, 300 mm. LEFT: 1/160 sec, f/6.3. RIGHT: 1/2 sec, f/18. Akaka Falls, HI.

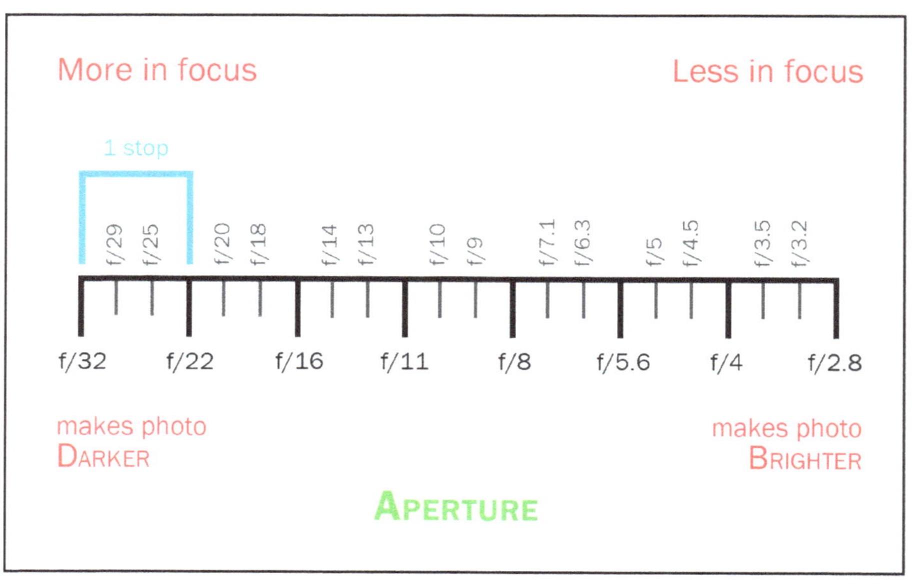

Table 4.3. Aperture.

Aperture

The aperture refers to the size of the lens opening that allows light to pass through to the sensor. It varies from wide to narrow and is dependent on the specific lens you are using. Below is a chart of possible f-stops you can choose (not all lenses will have all the settings listed). Those in bold are typical apertures available since the film era. They are one stop of exposure from the previous/next one in bold and either halves or doubles the amount of light. For example, an aperture set to f/11 lets in half as much light as f/8 but twice as much as f/16.

f/2.8 (wide)	f/3.2	f/3.5
f/4	f/4.5	f/5
f/5.6	f/6.3	f/7.1
f/8	f/9	f/10
f/11	f/13	f/14
f/16	f/18	f/20
f/22	f/25	f/29 (narrow)

Table 4.4. Aperture values (wide-narrow) from left to right.

A "fast" lens is determined by its maximum (or widest) aperture because the larger it can open, the faster the shutter speed you can use. An f/2.8 lens is faster than an f/4, for example.

The size of the opening in the lens determines the depth of field. **Depth of field (DOF)** is how much of the scene in front of and behind your subject is in focus. The small numbers (f/1.4 - f/4) represent larger openings and the least DOF. Large numbers (f/18 - f/32) have small openings and the greatest DOF. Another factor that affects the DOF is the focal length of the lens. Wide angle lenses naturally have more DOF, while telephoto lenses will have a much narrower DOF.

27 mm

f/5.6   f/22

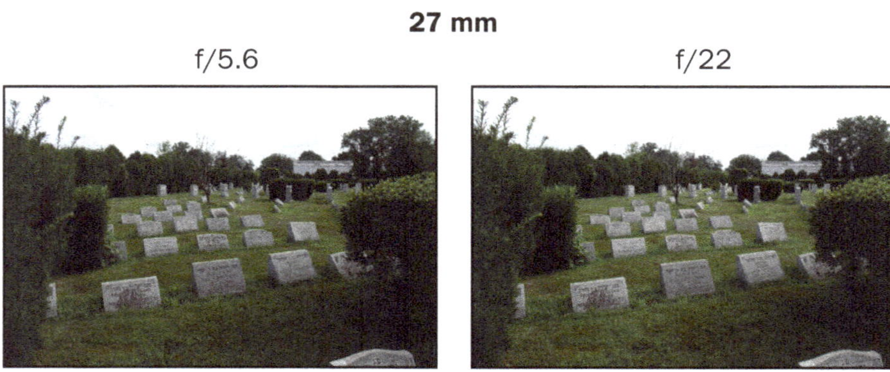

There is little noticeable difference in the depth of field at wide angles.

82 mm

f/5.6   f/22

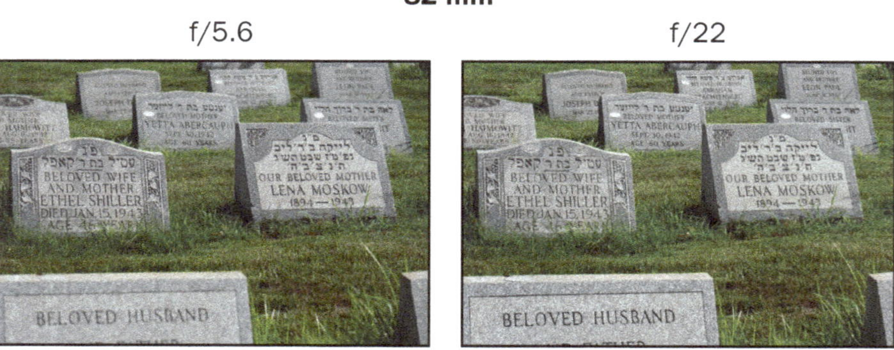

The differences become more obvious, especially in the foreground.

300 mm

f/5.6   f/22

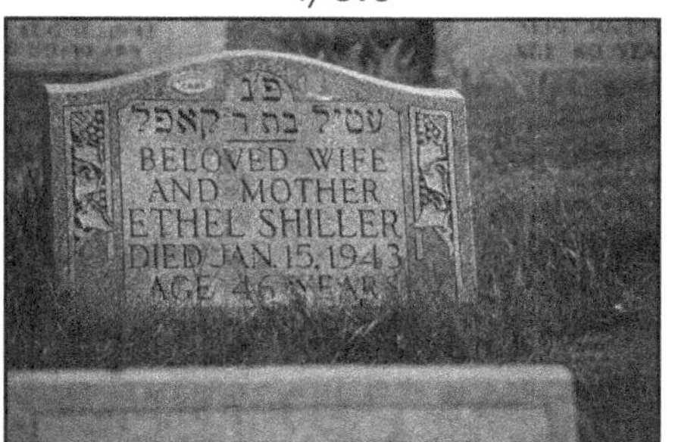
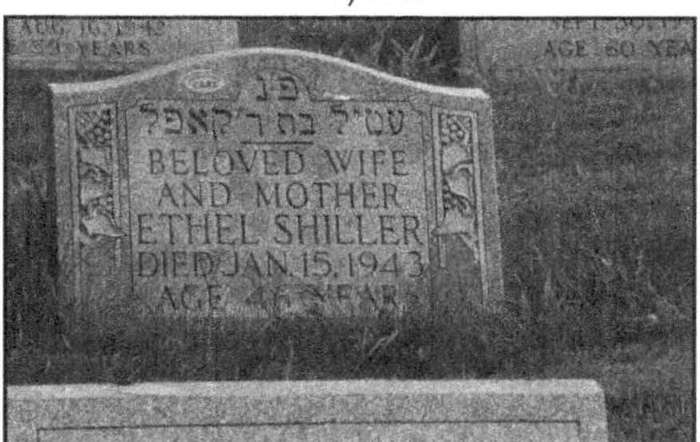

Stones in the foreground and background are blurry at f/5.6 and much sharper at f/22 with a long focal length.

450 mm

f/5.6   f/22

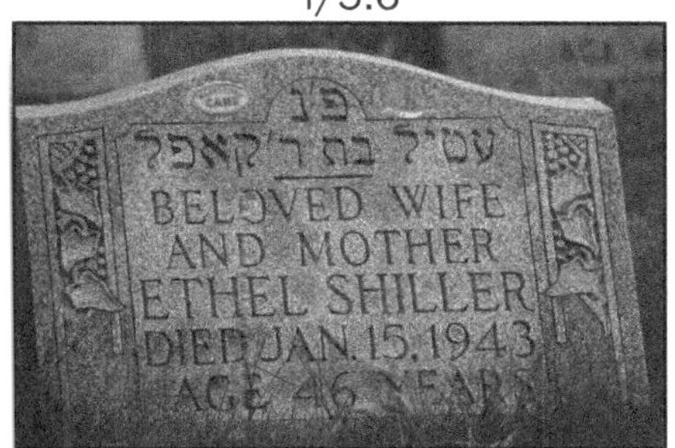
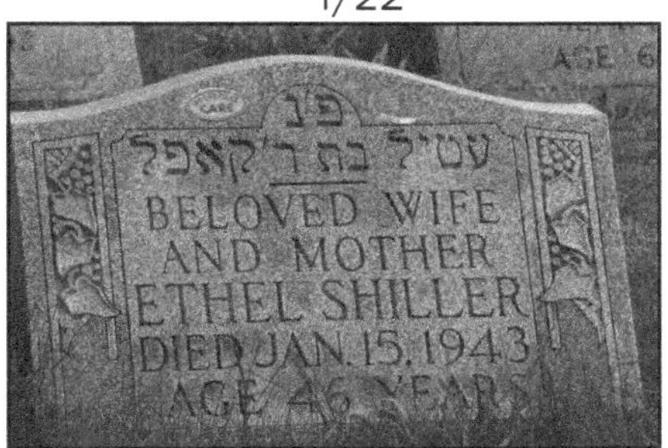

The stone in the background is barely legible at f/5.6 but you can see the word "AGE" at f/22.

ISO / ASA

If you remember the days of film, you may recall buying rolls that were rated 100, 200, 400, 800, or 1600 ASA. The lower the number, the more light you needed to make a good image. You used 100 or 200 outside on bright days, 400 if you expected to be indoors and outdoors with the same roll of film, and 1600 if you were going to shoot a school play or graduation in a dark auditorium.

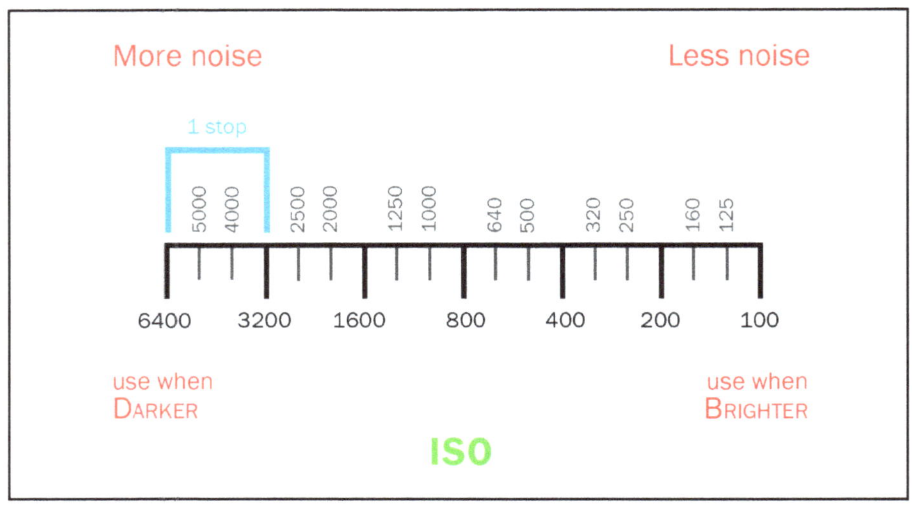

Table 4.5. ISO.

In digital photography, your camera uses a similar setting, now called ISO, as a measure of light sensitivity. The same principle is at work: lower numbers for bright shooting conditions and higher numbers for darker ones. What's nice here is that you no longer need to finish a roll of film to change the ISO; you can change it for each image, if you want.

Changing the ISO from 100 to 200 effectively changes your exposure by one stop. Each time the ISO doubles, you are adding another stop (gaining more light sensitivity, which allows for faster shutter speeds and/or smaller apertures).

The trade-off is in what we call digital noise (or grain, if we were using film). The higher number ISOs will tend to have more noise which looks like errant pixels in the midst of otherwise solid colors. Or bands of pixels that differ in brightness levels. You may notice it more in the shadows than highlights. You will get the best and smoothest results by keeping your ISO as low as possible. But sometimes, you just need to use a very high ISO of 1600, 3200, or higher to get the shot you want.

The image below was shot at a high ISO (1600) and you can start to see dark and light horizontal bands in the white areas of the horse's body.

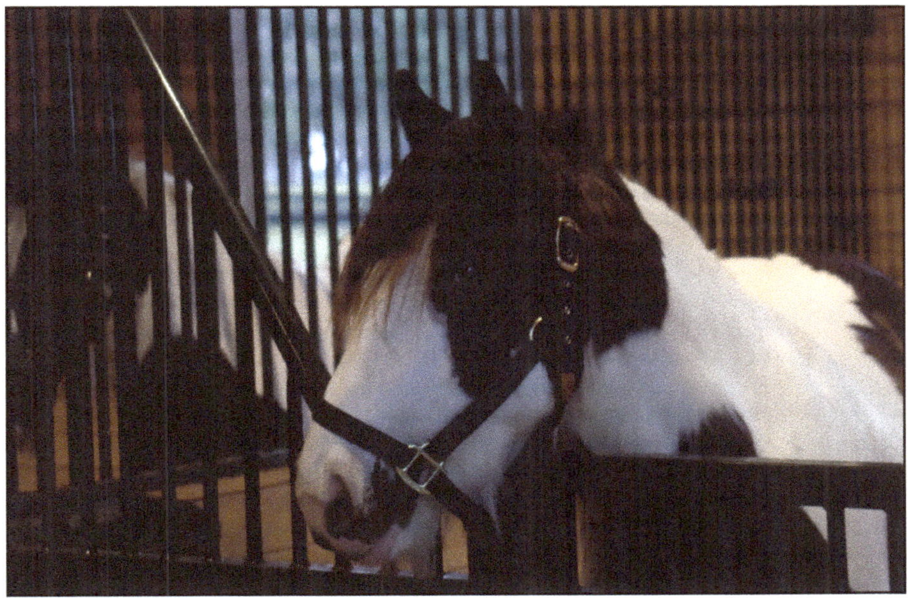

Minolta Maxxum 7D, shutter priority, pattern metering, 1/125 sec, f/4.5, ISO 1600, 90 mm. Ocala, FL.

Exposure Triangle

Changing one setting (whether shutter speed, f-stop, or ISO) affects the others and is referred to as the exposure triangle. There are multiple settings that will give you the same amount of exposure; however, you might prefer one setting over another, due to the effects those settings create.

If it's a sunny day, the correct exposure could be 1/100 sec and f/16 at ISO 100. (This is known as the "Sunny 16" rule and states that on a sunny day, at f/16, the shutter speed will be approximately the inverse of the ISO.) Each pair of shutter/ aperture settings below provides the same amount of exposure.

Shutter	1/1600	1/800	1/400	1/200	1/100	1/50	1/25
Aperture	f/4	f/5.6	f/8	f/11	f/16	f/22	f/32

Table 4.6. Sample exposure values at ISO 100.

As the f-stop moves a whole stop up (to the left, smaller

number, wider opening) or down (to the right, larger number, narrower opening), the shutter speed must double or halve, to maintain the same exposure. An aperture of f/4 is fairly wide, letting in a lot of light, which requires a fast shutter speed so as not to overexpose the image. This setting is appropriate if you're trying to freeze some action and/or you're trying to blur the background. Likewise, with a narrow aperture of f/32, the shutter needs to be open much longer to let in the same amount of light. This setting works well to create a larger depth of field and/or if some motion blur is desired (assuming you are photographing something on the move).

If we double the ISO to 200 from our example above, we are effectively adding more light sensitivity to the mix so at a given f/stop, you can use a faster shutter speed.

Shutter	1/3200	1/1600	1/800	1/400	1/200	1/100	1/50
Aperture	f/4	f/5.6	f/8	f/11	f/16	f/22	f/32

Table 4.7. Sample exposure values at ISO 200.

Histogram

The histogram is a graph of your image's exposure that looks like a mountain range. The left end is black and the right end is white. Ideally, you want your mountain range to be mostly in the middle rather than up against either end which would mean having a very dark or very bright image. If you get a lot of pixels that are either pure black or pure white, this is called "clipping" and indicates that there is no detail in the black or white areas (see "Blinkies," below). Once that happens, there is nothing you can do to reintroduce those details after you have taken the photo (even in image editing software).

The histogram is more accurate than reviewing your photo on the LCD screen since that can often be adjusted brighter or darker in your menu. Looking at a histogram immediately after taking the picture is a quick way to judge whether you need to adjust the exposure one way or the other. See the following examples.

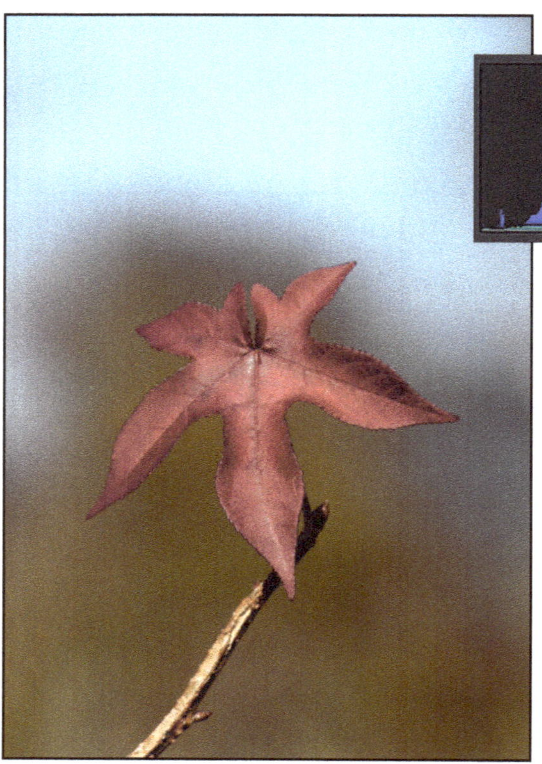

The histogram shows an image with a good balance of dark and bright pixels.

Sony A700, shutter priority, center-weighted metering, 1/640 sec, f/8, ISO 200, 450 mm. Morris Arboretum, Philadelphia, PA.

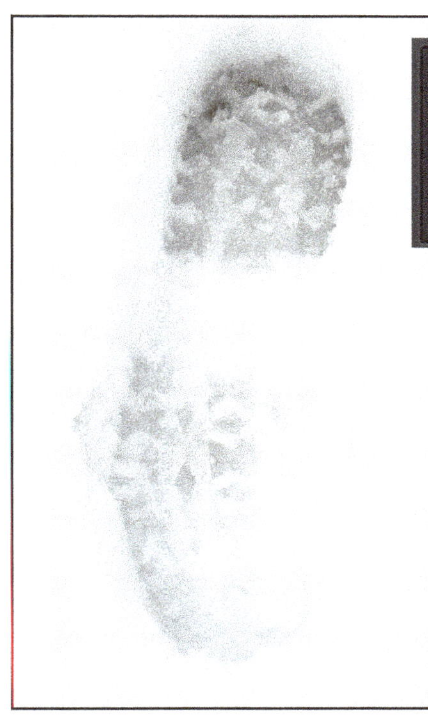

The histogram shows the image is very bright (graph shows most of the pixels on the right) with very few pixels that are mid-range to dark (on the left). This is to be expected since the snow is bright.

Boot print in snow. Nikon D3200, aperture priority, center-weighted metering, 1/160 sec, f/13, ISO 400, 82 mm. Glenside, PA.

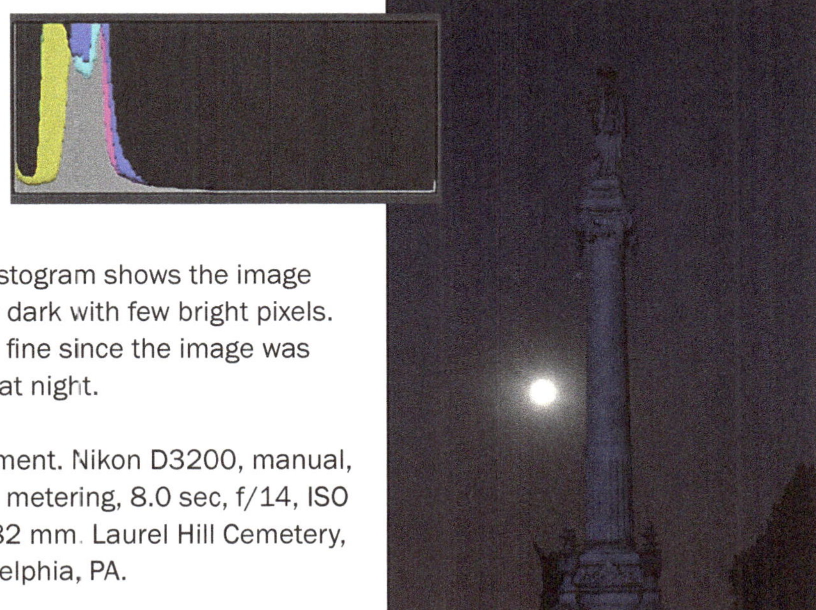

The histogram shows the image is very dark with few bright pixels. This is fine since the image was taken at night.

Monument. Nikon D3200, manual, matrix metering, 8.0 sec, f/14, ISO 400, 82 mm. Laurel Hill Cemetery, Philadelphia, PA.

Blinkies

Related to the histogram is a setting to show if your images have clipped either the black or white end of your exposure. The area affected "blinks" black/white to show where those areas are in your image so you can adjust your exposure accordingly. I find seeing where the highlights have turned completely white to be very helpful, especially when including the sky or water. You'll need to consult your manual for instructions on how to view this information.

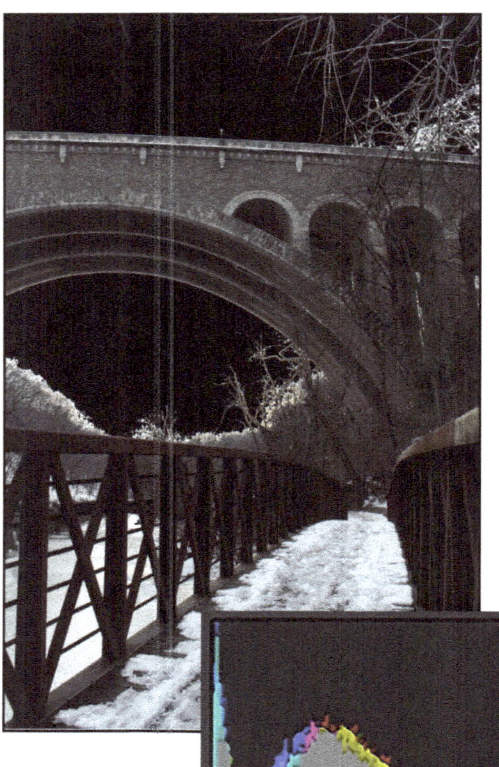

The sky is shown here in black to simulate what you would see on your camera's LCD screen because it was completely overexposed and pure white. The histogram below shows a large number of pure white pixels as well (circled in red).

Walnut Lane and pedestrian bridges. Nikon D3200, shutter priority, matrix metering, 1/250 sec, f/8, ISO 400, 27 mm. Along Wissahickon Avenue in Philadelphia, PA.

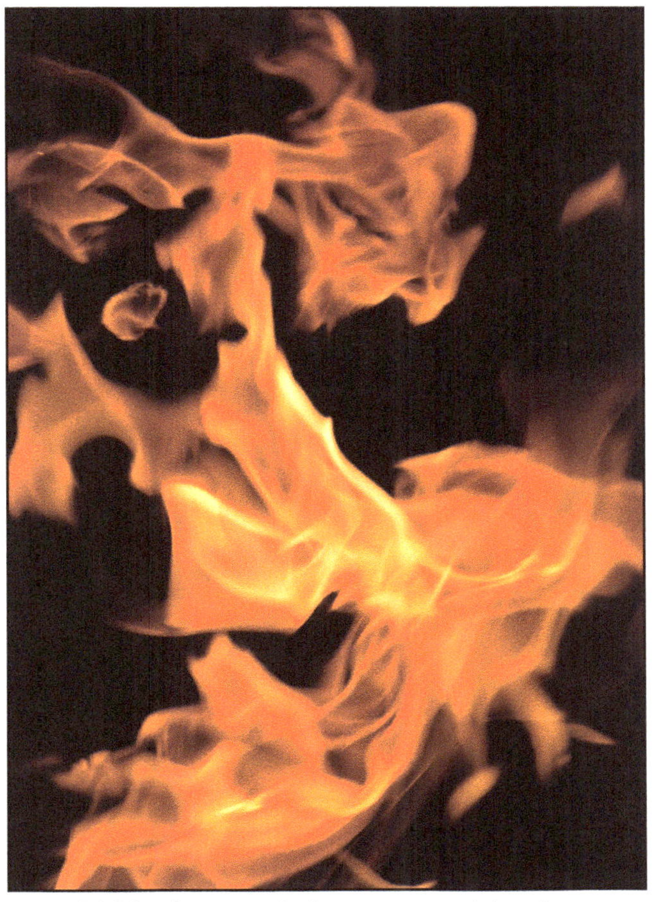

Fire pit. Nikon D3200, shutter priority, center-weighted average, 1/250 sec, f/4.8, ISO 100, -1 EV, 174 mm. Glenside, PA.

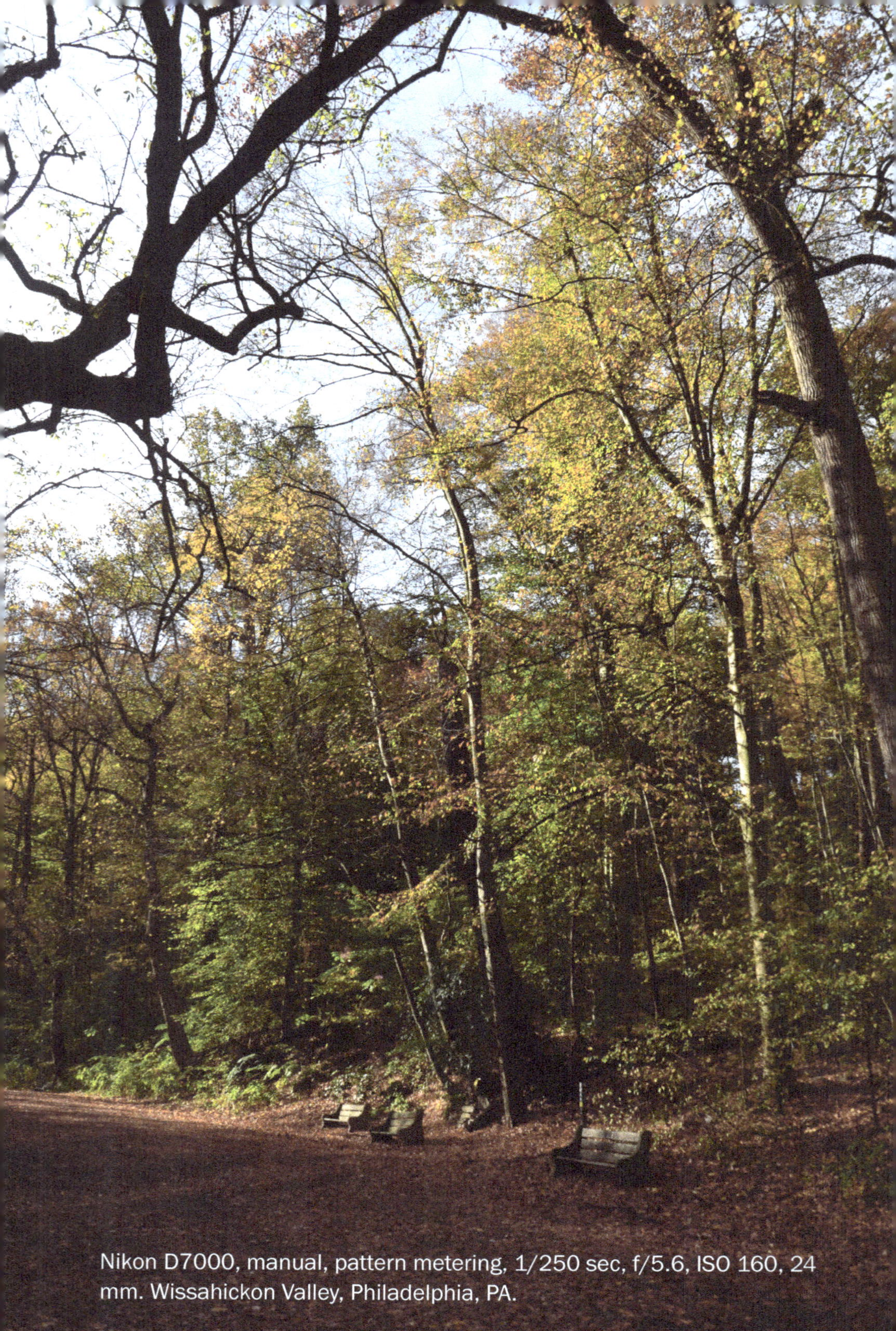

Nikon D7000, manual, pattern metering, 1/250 sec, f/5.6, ISO 160, 24 mm. Wissahickon Valley, Philadelphia, PA.

5.
Exposure Metering

Using an internal light meter, the camera will make various assumptions about the scene, including that the average amount of reflected light will be about 18% grey (which may or may not be an accurate assessment). You can set how your camera analyzes the scene. Common choices include matrix, center-weighted, partial, and spot. Consult your manual for directions on how to change the metering system your camera uses.

Matrix (also called *pattern*, *evaluative*, *multi*, *segment*, or *honeycomb*) metering considers the entire scene, using various zones and algorithms to determine "proper" exposure. This is a good mode for most situations where the lighting is fairly even across the scene.

Center-weighted metering is much like it sounds: while the meter will look at the entire scene, it gives much more consideration to the area in the center, defined rather broadly. This may give you better results if your subject is not in one of the corners and it's noticeably brighter or darker than the edges of the scene. It's good for portraits (since our subjects tend to be in the middle).

Spot and *partial* metering concentrate on the center of the image (or the active focus point, see the next chapter) and ignore all else. Use one of these if your subject is small and differs greatly in contrast from the rest of the scene. This is a setting for more advanced and professional photographers but definitely worth some experimentation for novices. Try this setting if your subject is lit from behind (backlit) and you don't want a silhouette. Or when shooting the moon at night, a very bright object surrounded by black sky.

Following are several examples of the same composition, using different metering modes.

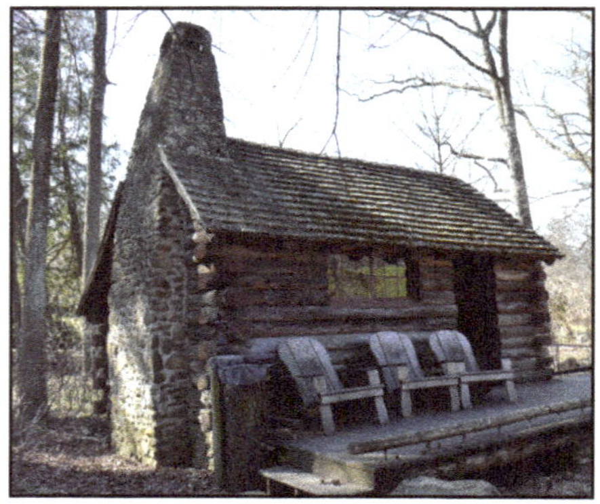

Matrix, 1/40 sec, f/8.

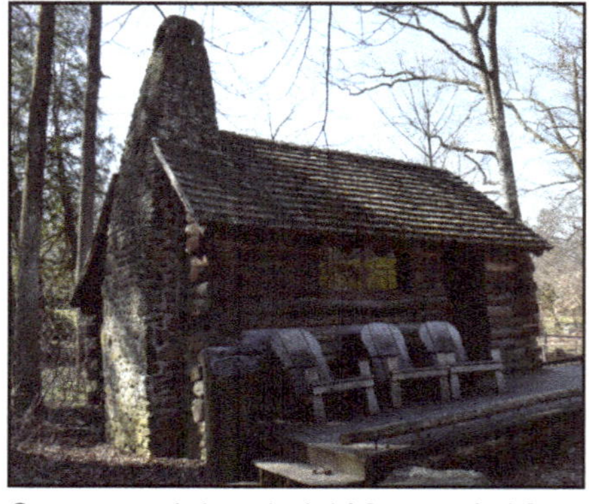

Center-weighted, 1/40 sec, f/10.

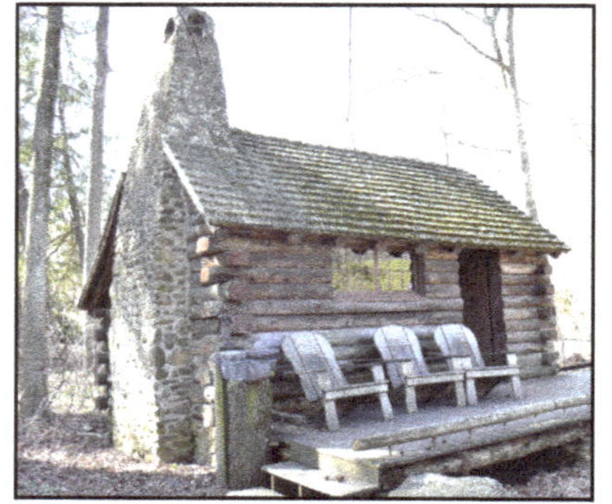

Spot, 1/40 sec, f/4.0.

**Matrix has the
best exposure.**

All images Nikon D3200, shutter priority, ISO 100, 27 mm. Log cabin at Morris Arboretum in Philadelphia.

40

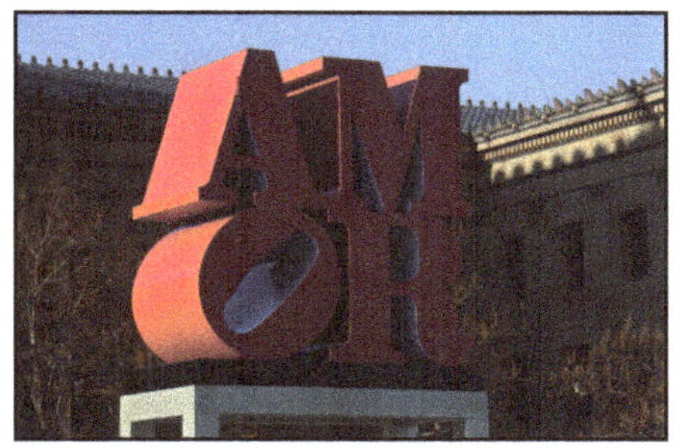

Matrix, 1/125 sec, f/13, 129 mm.

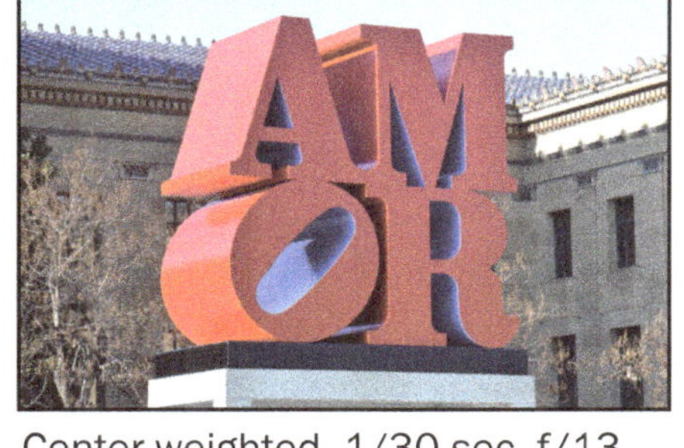

Center-weighted, 1/30 sec, f/13, 138 mm.

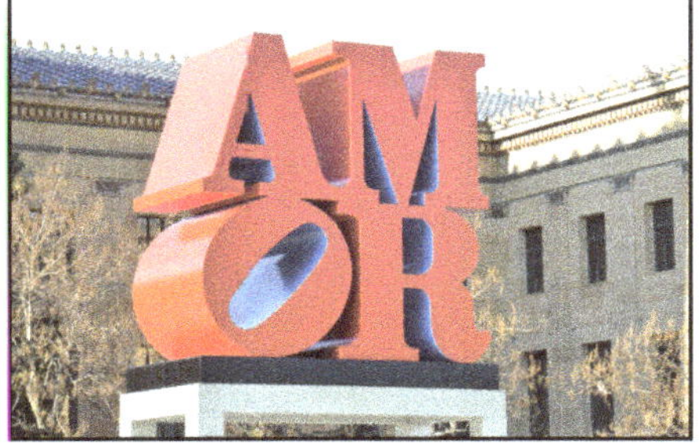

Spot, 1/20 sec, f/13, 129 mm.

Center-weighted has the best exposure.

All images: Nikon D3200, aperture priority, ISO 100. Amor statue at the Philadelphia Museum of Art.

Matrix, 1/20 sec, f/5.6.

Center-weighted, 1/160 sec, f/5.6.

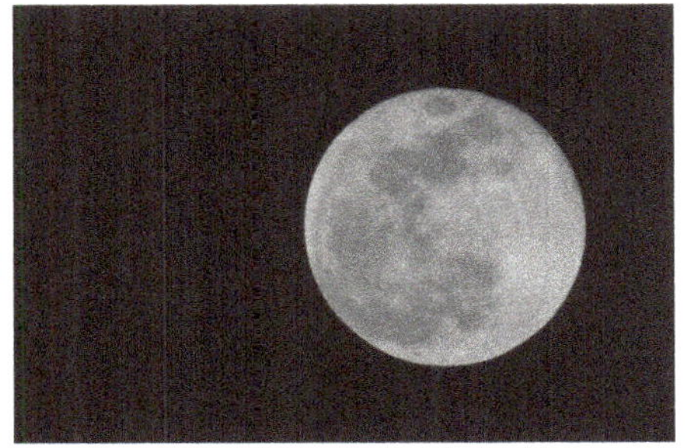

Spot, 1/800 sec, f/5.6.

Spot has the best exposure.

All images: Nikon D3200, aperture priority, ISO 200, -0.3 EV, 450 mm.

Exposure Lock

If there is a big contrast in the scene and your subject is either much brighter or much darker than its surroundings, you can use the exposure lock function of your camera in conjunction with spot metering, especially if you'd like to put your subject off center. Exposure lock works by taking an exposure reading somewhere in the scene and then lets you recompose without losing those settings.

The following directions may or may not be similar to your own (check your manual to get specific directions for your camera). Many brands have a button with AE-L or AE abbreviation. Focus on the spot where you'd like to take the exposure reading (usually the brightest area) by pressing the shutter button halfway down. Now press and hold the AE-L or AE button, let go of the shutter, and recompose the shot, keeping the AE-L button pressed until you take the photo.

⊞ *Exposure Compensation*

One way to discuss proper exposure is through Exposure Values, or EV (see page 23). Since shutter speed, aperture, and ISO all use different units, EV makes it a little easier to express your exposures. The "proper" exposure is expressed as 0 EV. Keep in mind that correct exposure could be any number of combinations of shutter, aperture, and ISO that all let in the same amount of light, as discussed in the previous chapter.

Despite your best efforts in choosing the proper shutter speed and/or aperture, your image may need some adjusting to increase or decrease the exposure. One way to make adjustments is by using exposure compensation. Check your manual to see what range your camera has available: +/- 2, +/- 3, or +/- 5 stops are common. You may be able to change in 1/3 or 1/2-stop increments. Adjustments in 1/3-stop scale include -2, -1-2/3 (-1.7), -1-1/3 (-1.3), -1, -2/3 (-0.7), -1/3 (-0.3), +1/3 (+0.3), +2/3 (+0.7), +1, +1-1/3 (+1.3), +1-2/3 (+1.7), and +2.

The positive end of the compensation adds light to your exposure. Use this when your image is too dark or when white snow looks grey in the photo.

The negative end takes away light from your exposure, making it darker. Use this when everything is too bright or your black areas aren't black enough.

How do you know how much to adjust your exposure? There is no true guideline here; trial and error as well as experience are your best teachers. Try little tweaks of 1/3 or 2/3 in the desired direction (positive or negative) and see if you like the results. If you really need to go as far as +/- 3 EV, you may want to change the ISO, shutter, or aperture first.

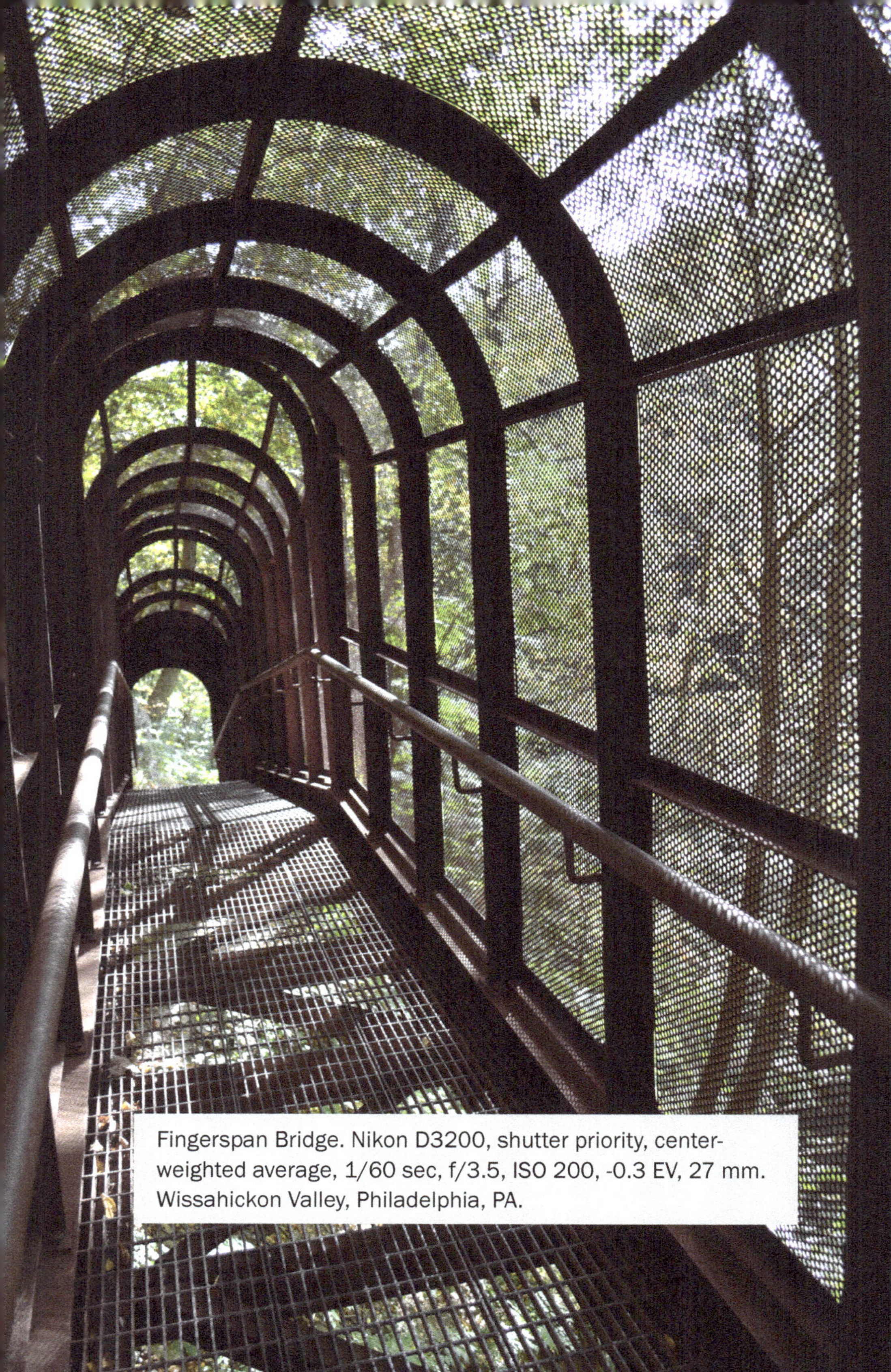

Fingerspan Bridge. Nikon D3200, shutter priority, center-weighted average, 1/60 sec, f/3.5, ISO 200, -0.3 EV, 27 mm. Wissahickon Valley, Philadelphia, PA.

Bracketing

Bracketing is a series of photos of the same scene with different exposures. If the scene you're shooting varies widely in exposure values with some deep shadows and bright highlights, take several shots: one at the correct meter reading, at least one that is overexposed to get detail in the shadows, and at least one that is underexposed to get detail in the highlight areas. (Some cameras may do this automatically, check your manual for specific instructions.) Later, you can combine the three (or more) images in your image editing software of choice. It's up to you how much you want to compensate in each direction. And since it's digital, you can experiment all you want and delete whichever shots aren't needed.

LEFT: 1/60 sec, underexposed (-1.7 EV). BOTTOM: 1/20 sec, metered exposure.

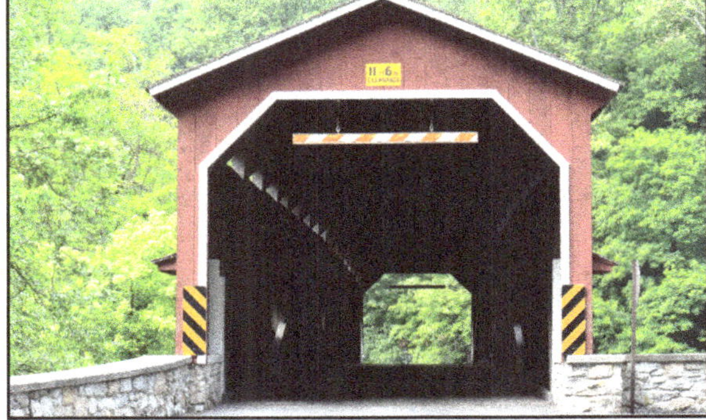

Nikon D7000, aperture priority, pattern metering, f/14, ISO 400, 82 mm. Pequea, PA.

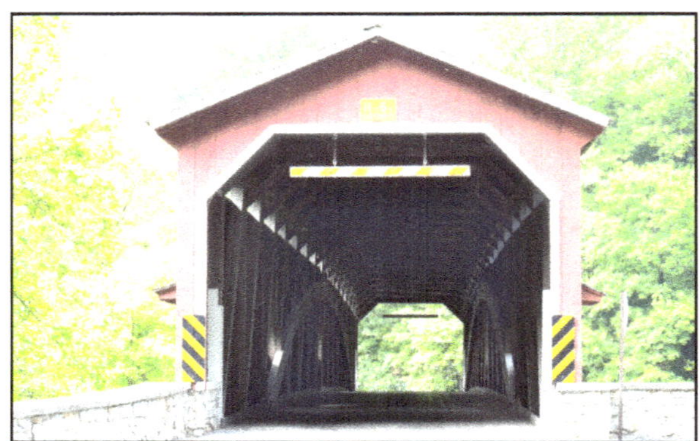

1/6 sec, overexposed
(+1.7 EV).

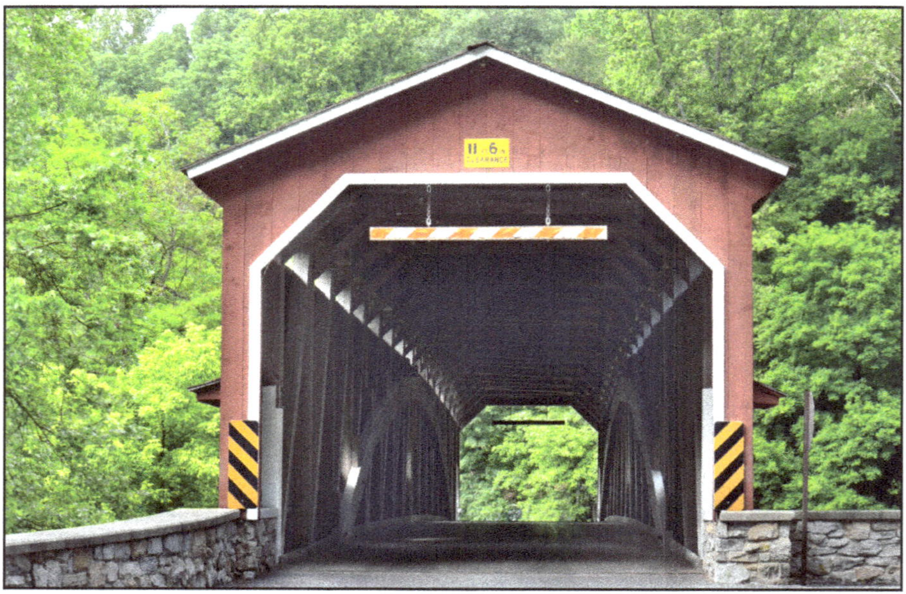

I combined the previous images to create the one above. The underexposed image had the best stone wall and vibrant trees. The metered exposure provided the bridge exterior and the greenery at the far side. The overexposed image provided the bridge interior.

This is a technique called High Dynamic Range or HDR.

6.

Focusing

The camera will start to focus when you press the shutter button down halfway. Once in focus, to take the picture, press the button down completely. If you're new to digital photography, you may need to practice a bit to get used to the feel and timing.

Focus Mode

The focus mode tells the camera if you expect to be photographing stationary or moving subjects. This can help the camera to focus faster. (Names are listed by Canon / Nikon terminology.)

One-Shot/Single-servo: For stationary subjects. The camera will lock focus when the shutter button is halfway pressed.

AI Servo/Continuous-servo: For moving subjects. The camera continuously focuses while the shutter button is halfway pressed.

AI Focus/Auto-servo: The camera automatically chooses between one-shot/single-servo (if the subject is stationary) and AI servo/continuous-servo for moving subjects.

AF-Area Mode/Focus Points

You may have noticed a number of small squares/rectangles/circles when you look through the viewfinder. The default setting is to focus on the center point, regardless of where your subject is actually located. If you'd like your subject to be off-center, focus on your subject first by putting the subject in the center and pressing the shutter button halfway. Keeping the shutter halfway down, recompose the photo, putting your subject where you want it. Take the picture by pushing the shutter button down all the way.

Alternatively, you can set one of the other points for your camera to use rather than the one in the center or allowing your camera to decide where the subject is.

Canon gives you two options: Manual AF Point Selection and Automatic AF Point Selection. In **Manual AF Point Selection**, you choose the point and that's where the camera will focus when you press the shutter button. In **Automatic AF Point Selection**, the camera considers all focusing points and will generally choose the point(s) over the object(s) closest to the lens.

Nikon gives you four options: auto-area AF, single-point AF, dynamic-area AF, and 3D-tracking. In **auto-area AF**, the camera chooses the focus point(s) based on the subject (usually the closest object). **Single-point AF** lets you choose the one point to use for focusing (best for stationary subjects). **Dynamic-**

area AF allows you to set a focus point but the camera can use information from the surrounding focus points if the subject briefly leaves the selected point to maintain focus. **3D-tracking AF** is available only in continuous or auto-servo modes (see above). You set the focus point and if the subject moves after the camera has focused, it will use 3D-tracking to select a new focus point and keep the focus locked on the original subject as long as the shutter button is pressed halfway.

Consult your manual for directions on setting your own focal point as each camera manufacturer differs in this regard. **Note:** if you're shooting in Auto, and possibly any of the other auto modes (portrait, sports, landscape, etc., see Chapter 8), you may not be able to choose the focus points (the center point will be used).

There are several situations which are difficult for your camera's auto focus:

- Little to no contrast between the subject and the background.
- The focus point includes objects at different distances (such as an animal in a cage).
- The subject includes large areas of regular geometric patterns.
- The focus point includes a subject of sharp contrast (half in shadow/half in bright light).
- Something in the background is larger than the subject (building, tree, etc.)
- The subject is made up of many small details.

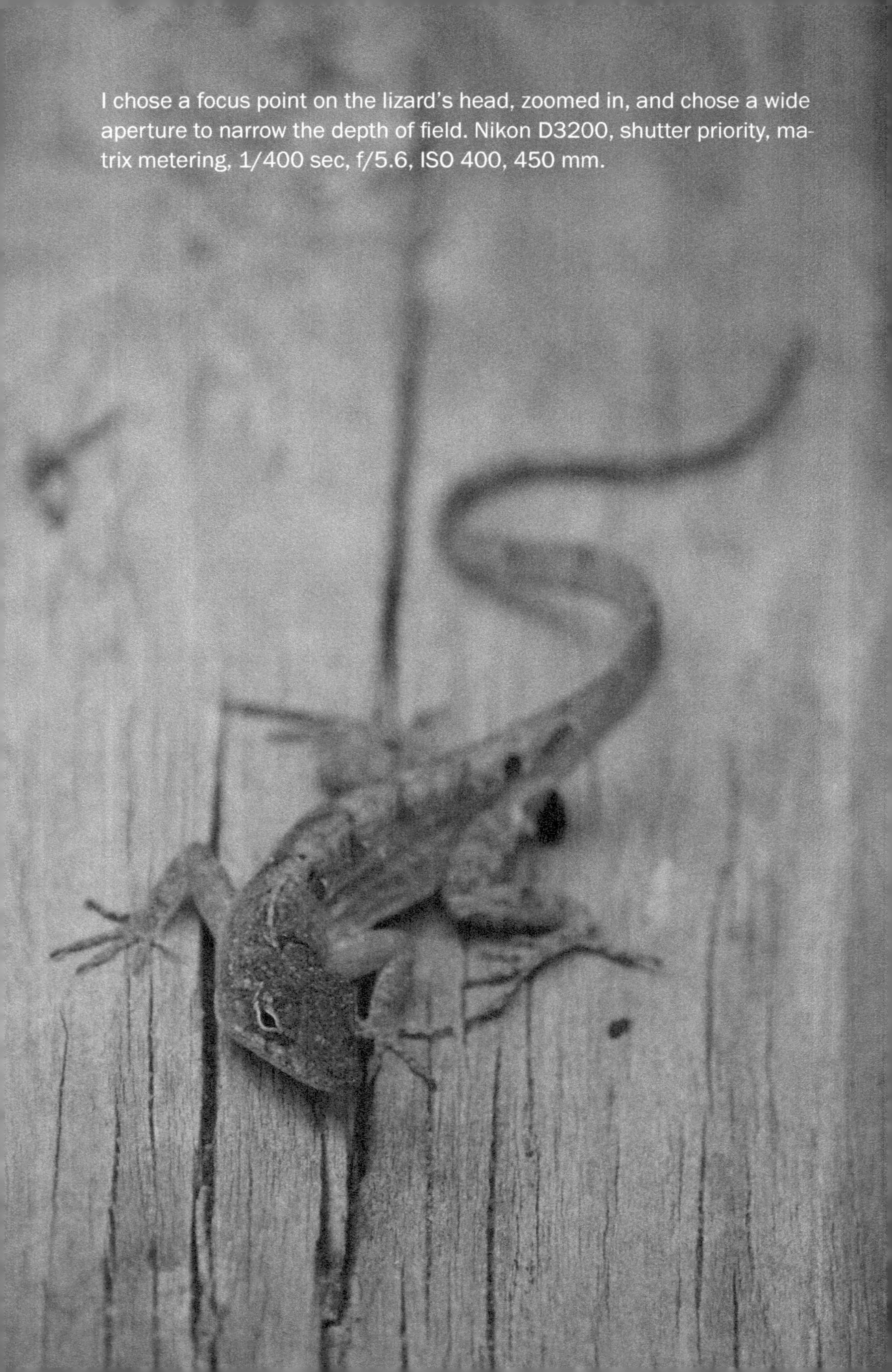

I chose a focus point on the lizard's head, zoomed in, and chose a wide aperture to narrow the depth of field. Nikon D3200, shutter priority, matrix metering, 1/400 sec, f/5.6, ISO 400, 450 mm.

When your camera is having difficulty focusing, you will hear the motor move back and forth as it tries to get a lock on the subject. Try switching the focus point or recomposing the image. If it's dark, you can try shining a flashlight onto your subject to assist your camera. And if none of these suggestions work, use manual focus (often a switch on the side of the lens or the camera: AF/MF. AF stands for auto focus while MF stands for manual focus.)

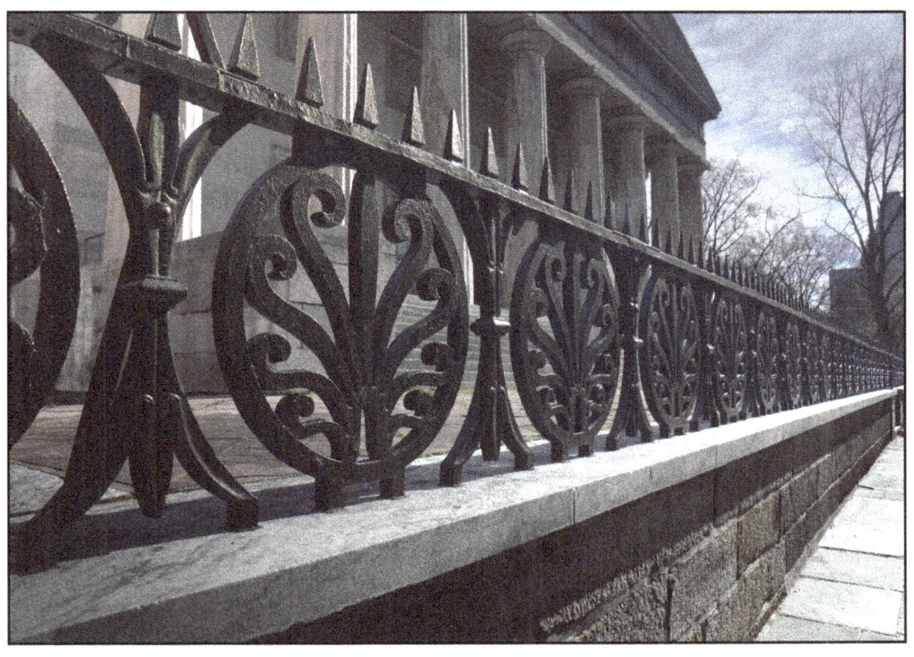

Railing. Nikon D3200, aperture priority, center-weighted average, 1/5 sec, f/5, ISO 100, with variable ND filter, 24 mm. Philadelphia, PA.

7.

White Balance

One of the many things I never learned until I took up digital photography was that light sources not only had particular colors associated with them, but also had measurable temperatures in degrees Kelvin. Our eyes are just so amazing that regardless of light source, we still see white as white.

The camera isn't that smart and needs to be told what's white or it will make its best guess in Auto **AWB**.

In addition to Auto, you will find presets for fluorescent, incandescent (or tungsten), sun, cloud, shade, and custom white balance. Check your camera's manual for information about which settings you have and how to change it.

Sunny ☀

Use when you are outside on a sunny day.

Cloudy ☁

Cloudy days are bluer than sunny ones. This setting counters the blue tint by adding some yellow, warming it up a bit.

Shady 🏠

Shade is bluer than the shadows created by clouds so this setting adds more yellow than the Cloudy setting.

Fluorescent

Fluorescent lights tend to be greenish or greenish-yellow. Using this setting will add magenta.

Incandescent/Tungsten

The old household bulbs tended to be yellow or orange. This setting adds blue.

Flash

Your built-in flash has its own color and if you're using it a lot, this may be a good setting to choose.

Custom/Preset

If the other settings aren't accurate, try a custom white balance. Consult your manual for directions. Most cameras require you to fill the image with something white or grey and take a picture of it. The camera analyzes that image and comes up with the white balance to use, based on temperature in degrees Kelvin.

> **ASIDE:** Most print film was daylight balanced so when you shot outside, the colors were perfect. When you came inside and didn't use the flash, colors generally weren't so great. Remember getting pictures back that were orange, green, or blue? Now you know why.

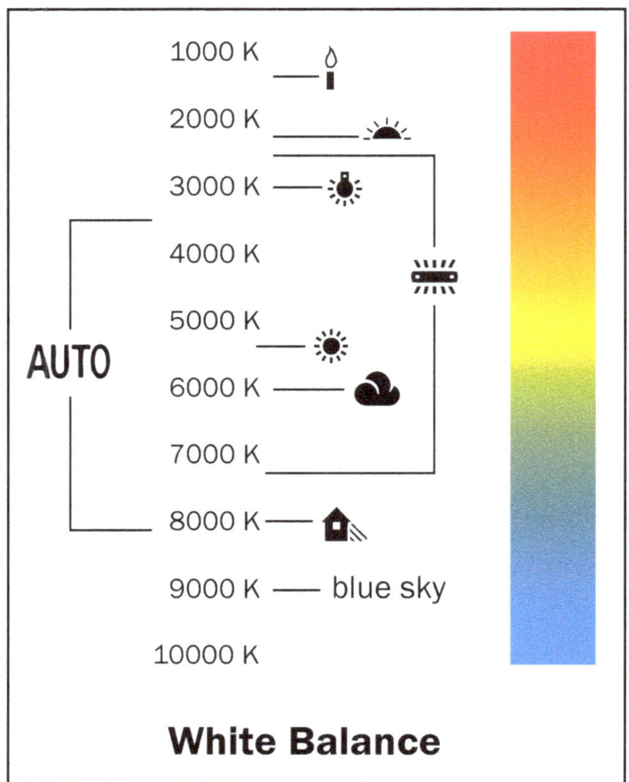

Figure 7-1. White balance scale in degrees Kelvin. Candlelight is the most red, followed by sunrise/sunset, household incandescent/tungsten bulbs are more orange, the sun is yellow, clouds and shade move into the blue part of the spectrum, while blue sky is obviously very blue. The temperature of fluorescent light has a wide range of possibilities.

Auto covers a good range but using auto with candlelight, sunrise/sunset, or a predominantly blue sky may result in images with an unexpected color cast.

The following snowy scene was photographed with different white balances. Auto did a pretty nice job, actually. The cloudy setting might also be a good choice.

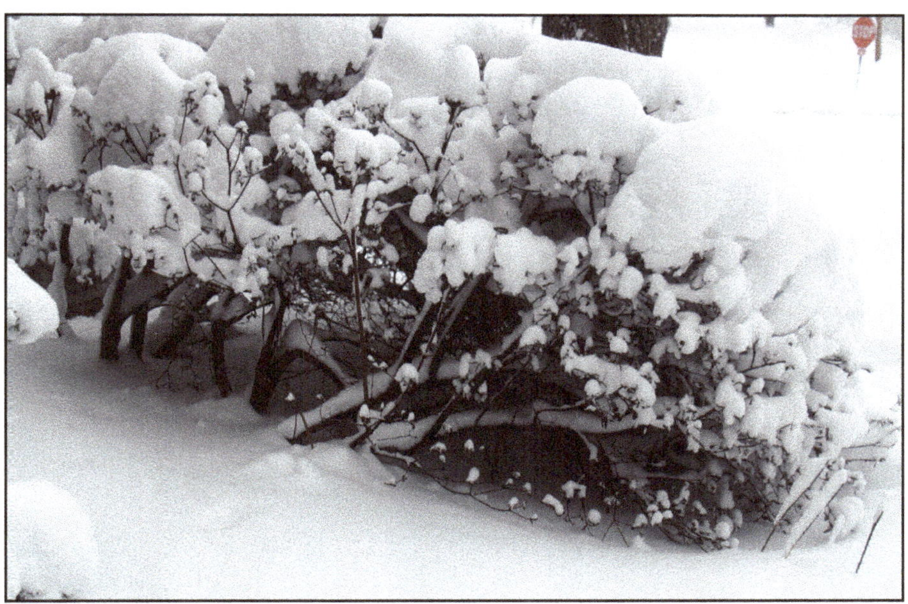

TOP: auto white balance; not bad. BOTTOM: white balance set to sun-shine. I find this a little too blue for my taste.

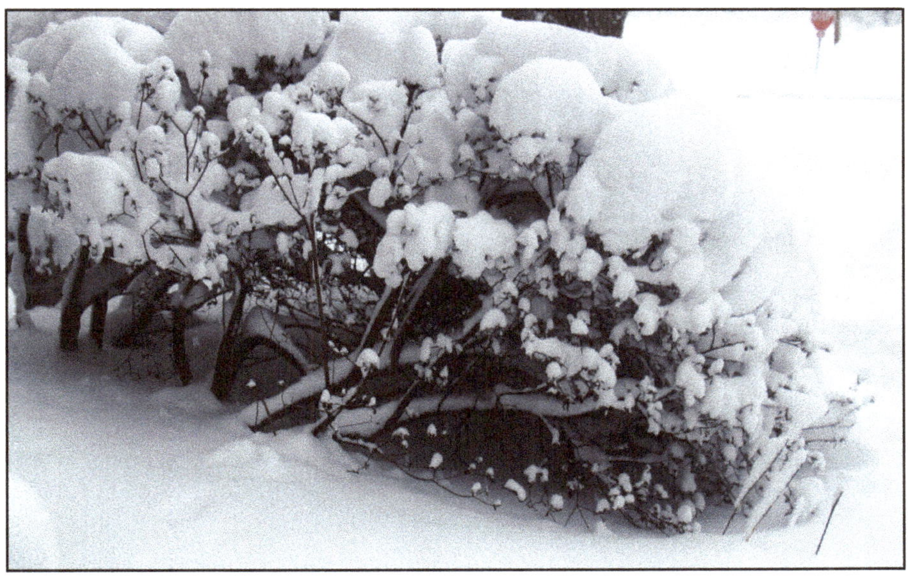

All photos: Minolta Maxxum 7D, shutter priority, pattern metering, 1/250 sec, f/6.7, ISO 100, 45 mm.

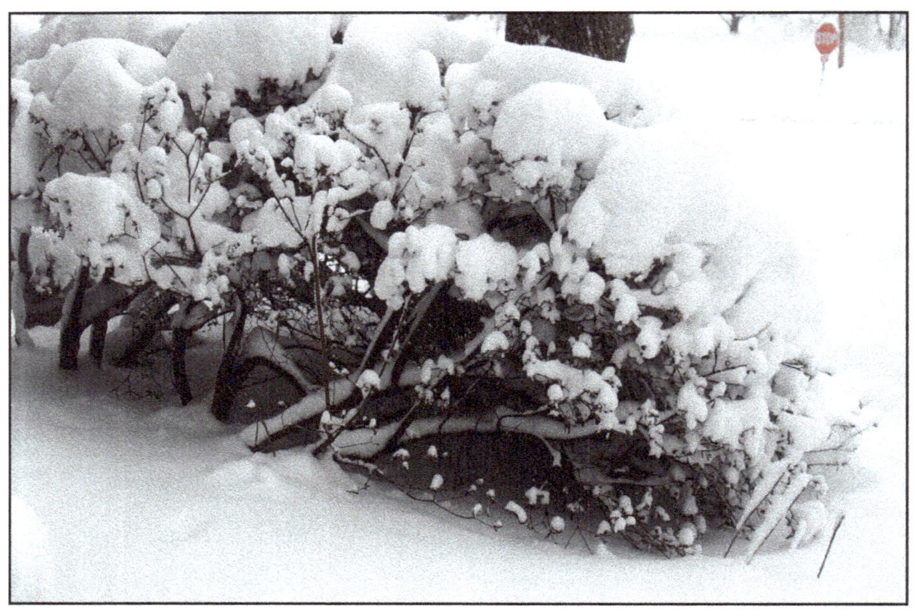

White balance set to cloudy. This is a pretty accurate rendition of the scene.

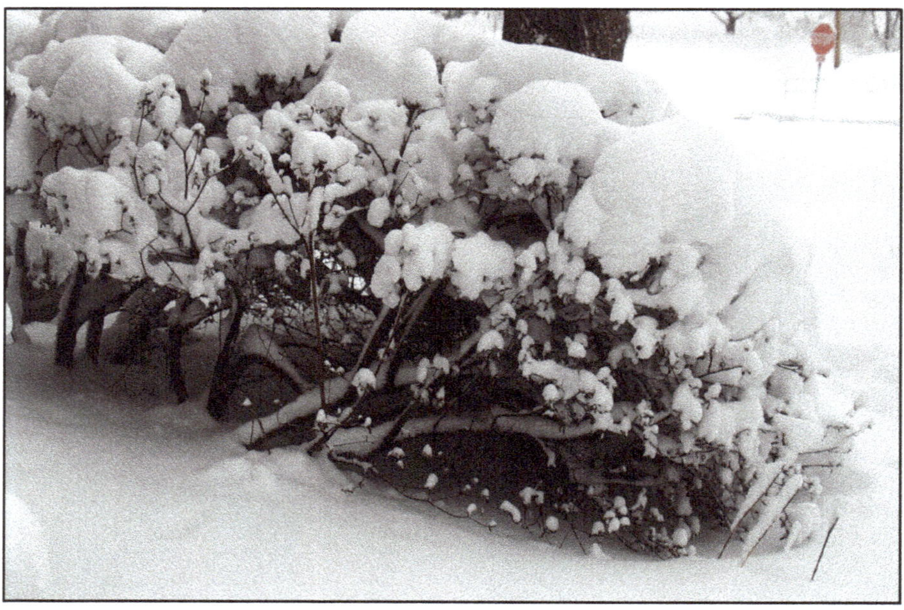

White balance set to shady. This adds more yellow than the cloudy setting above.

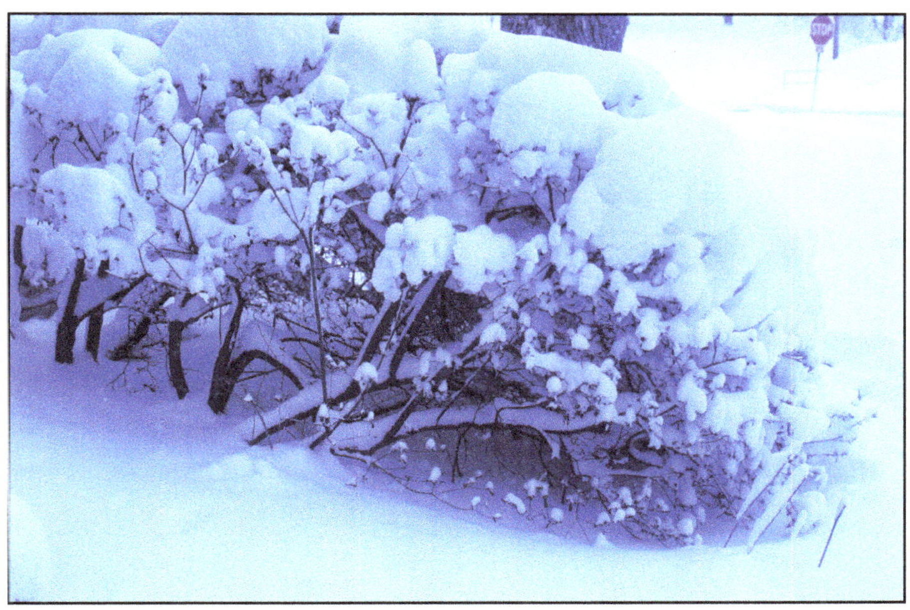

White balance set to tungsten turns the snow blue.

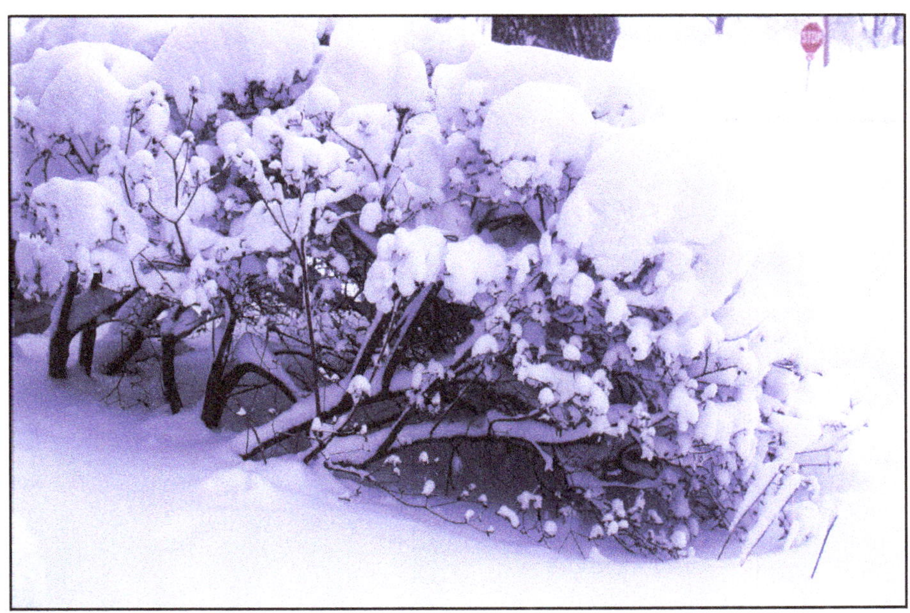

White balance set to fluorescent adds magenta/purple.

In more practical terms, you may be out and about shooting with your white balance set to auto and take a photo where the colors don't look like what you're seeing. Now it's time to experiment with some of the other options.

Below is a photo I took while in the woods and since the trees are full of leaves, it's very shady. The first image is with auto white balance and it's looking too blue. I changed the white balance to shade in the next image and that's too warm with yellow/red. The last image is set to cloudy which is still a little warm, but better than the other two, in my opinion.

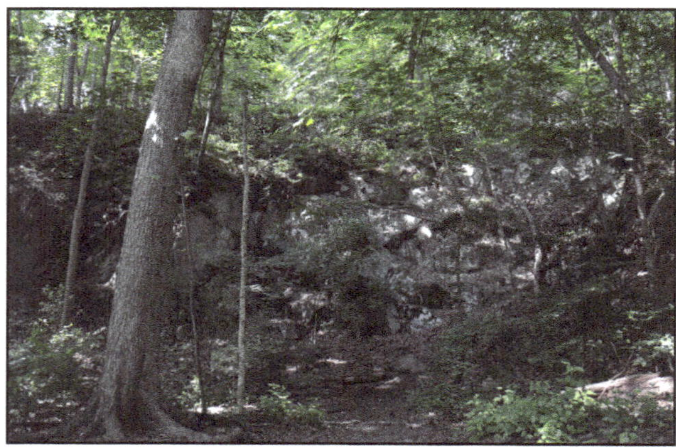

White balance set to Auto: too blue.

White balance set to Shade: too yellow/ red.

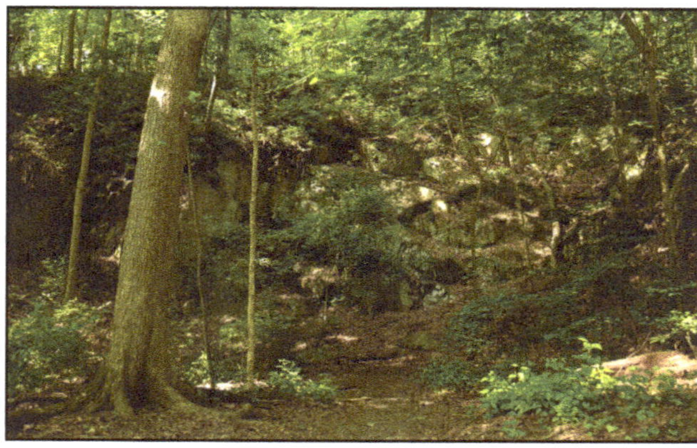

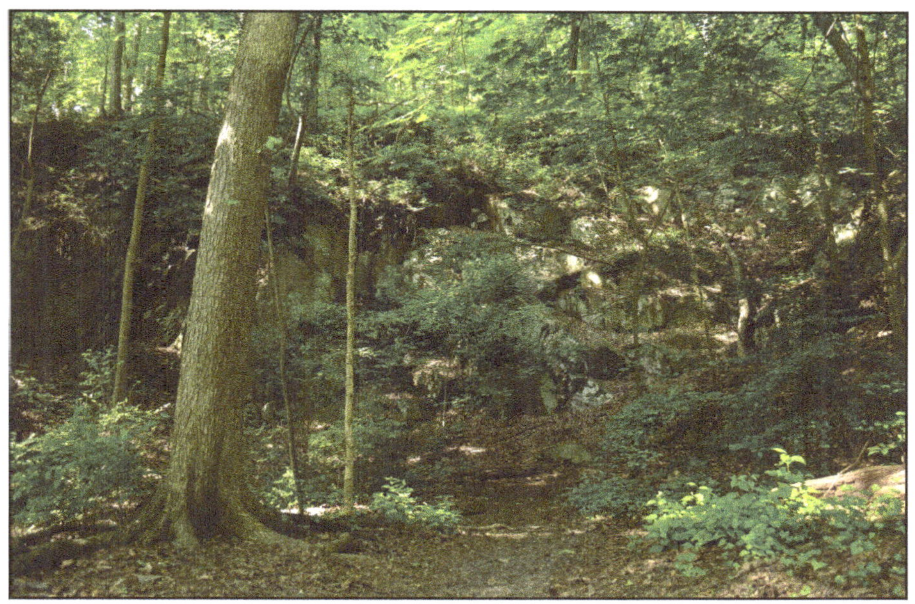

White balance set to Cloudy: definitely better, though still a bit yellow.

All images: Nikon D3200, aperture priority, pattern metering, f/3.5, ISO 400, -0.3 EV, 27 mm. First image: 1/80 sec; second and third images: 1/60 sec. Valley Green/Fairmount Park, Philadelphia, PA.

8.

Automatic Scene Modes

If you're new to digital photography, it can be difficult to know

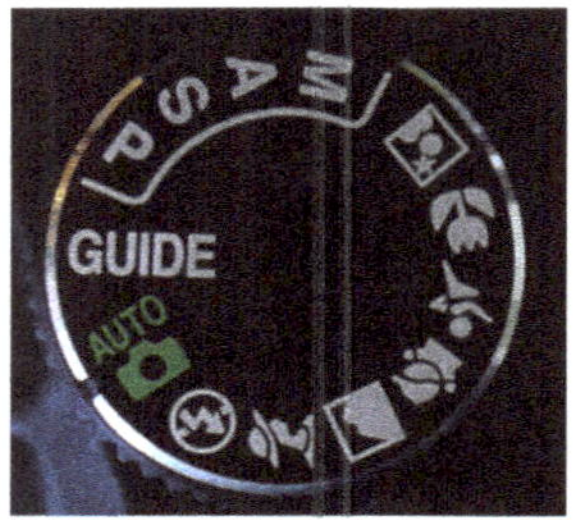

where to start. Many cameras come with several automatic modes where you can basically point and shoot. All of the exposure settings will be taken care of behind the scenes so you don't need to think about much besides composition.

Auto

You are in charge of composition only; your camera will make all of the decisions regarding exposure, flash, ISO, and white balance. Think of your DSLR as a big point-and-shoot. The camera will choose middle-of-the-road settings, generally, with shutter speeds that tend toward the slower end and apertures that aren't very wide or narrow.

Portrait

Are you taking pictures of a person? Or a single subject that you want to see pretty clearly? Choosing the portrait setting tells your camera to choose some different settings than Auto such as wider apertures (to blur the background) and pleasant skin tones. Check your manual to see what other adjustments your camera makes in this mode.

Landscape 

Instead of choosing wide apertures to blur the background, narrow apertures will bring more of the scene into focus by increasing the depth of field (see page 29). Colors, especially green and blue, may look more vibrant. The flash is likely unavailable, even if the lighting is poor. Consult your manual for other setting differences.

Sports

This mode is preferred to better freeze any action (it doesn't have to be sports-related). The camera chooses higher shutter speeds than when on Auto. The flash probably will not be available in this mode, either. Read your manual for other setting differences.

Kids

According to the manual for the Nikon D3200, this mode renders vivid clothing and background details but soft and natural skin tones, a mix of portrait and sports. Read your manual for other setting differences.

Macro

Use this setting when you're trying to get close-ups of smaller subjects, such as flowers, jewelry, coins, small toys, etc. If you have a zoom lens, the camera may have a hard time focusing when you are at the longest focal length (such as 200 mm or 300 mm). If that's a problem, pull your lens back to a smaller focal length. If you do a lot of macro photography, consider investing in a macro lens (these tend to be a fixed focal length, rather than

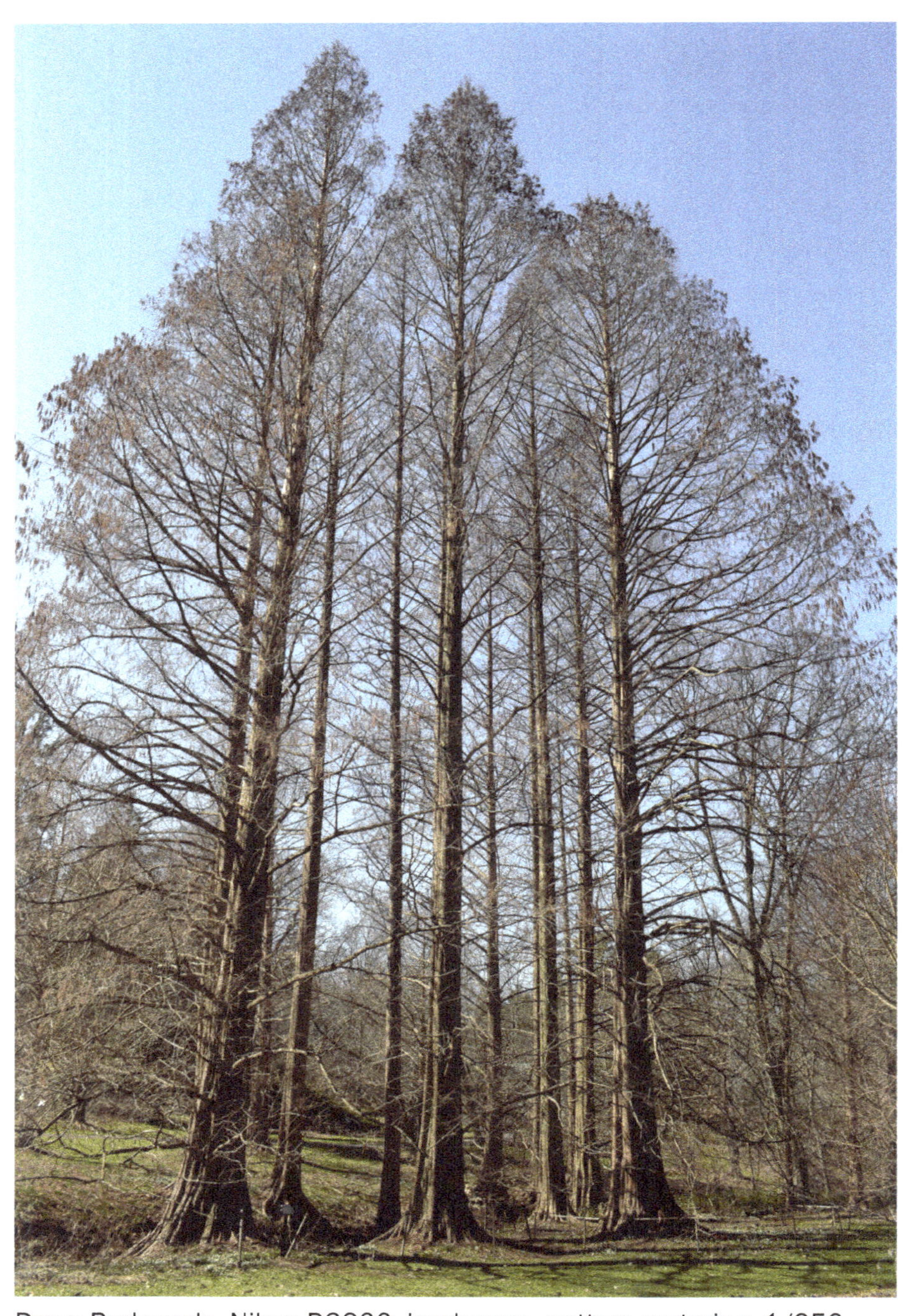

Dawn Redwoods. Nikon D3200, landscape, pattern metering, 1/250 sec, f/5.6, ISO 100, 27 mm. Morris Arboretum, Philadelphia, PA.

a zoom), that will have better glass and optical components. Using a tripod is recommended.

Night Portrait 

When you're taking pictures of people at night, this is worth trying. You will want to put your camera on something that won't move, such as a tripod or table, because the camera will use slow shutter speeds and then set off the flash at the end of the exposure.

Note: Point-and-shoot cameras often have even more scene modes than these, such as aquarium/underwater, cuisine, candle light, fireworks, party, beach/snow, aerial photo, and document/text.

> **ASIDE:** For a beginner, these might be worth using until you feel more comfortable with shutter speed, aperture, ISO, and the other settings that you can choose, instead of leaving those decisions to your camera. This section is included for informational purposes as I generally do not use these settings.

9.

Creative Camera Modes

If you want to take your camera off of Auto and the related scene modes, these are the settings to use. Here's where you truly get to take control (with the exception of Program/Creative Auto).

Program/Creative Auto

This is an "advanced auto" mode. You'll get somewhat more control with features such as flash, ISO, and white balance. The camera will still determine the shutter and aperture to use but you may be able to tweak it using the control dial or with exposure compensation settings (see page 42).

Shutter Priority (S or Tv)

You set the shutter speed, the camera chooses the aperture. You can also change settings for metering, flash, ISO, white balance, and exposure compensation. Choose this setting when you're working with subjects on the move. Slower shutter speeds will blur the action; faster shutter speeds will freeze the action. Remember that faster shutter speeds will need wider apertures or a higher ISO to avoid really dark images.

Aperture Priority (A or Av)

You set the aperture; the camera determines the shutter speed. You can also change settings for metering, flash, ISO, white balance, and exposure compensation. Use this setting to control the depth of field (how much of the scene is in focus in front of and behind your subject). Wide apertures (small numbers) tend to blur the background while narrow apertures (large numbers) keep more of the scene in focus. Keep in mind that narrow apertures don't allow as much light in through the lens so longer shutter speeds (and perhaps a tripod) will be necessary to obtain greater DOF.

Manual (M)

You have control over everything: shutter speed, aperture, metering, flash, ISO, and white balance. Use manual for complete artistic oversight, when you're experimenting, or shooting under complex situations. Consult your camera's manual for instructions on how to individually change the shutter and aperture.

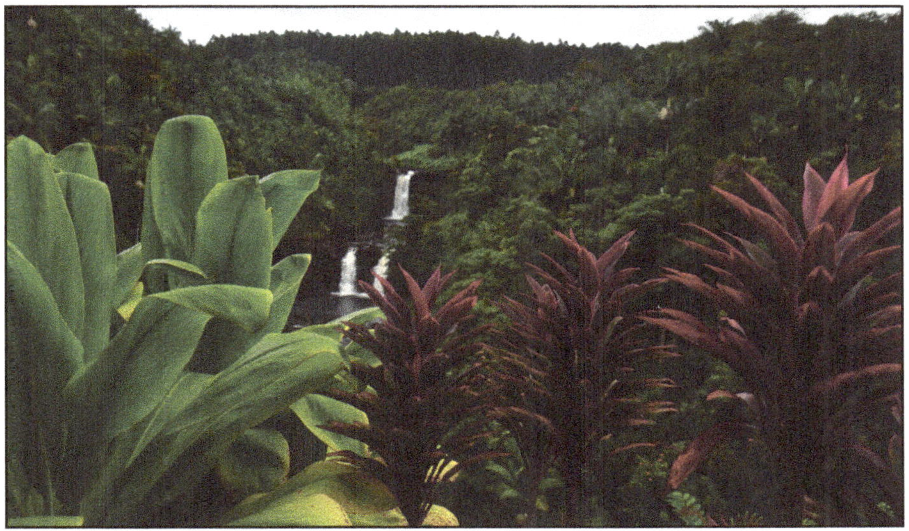

Umauma Falls. Nikon D7000, manual, matrix metering, 1/160 sec, f/7.1, ISO 400, 39 mm. Hawaii.

10.

Get the Shot

Now that you're ready to take control of your photography with shutter priority, aperture priority, or manual, it's time to discuss what's possible and how to make it happen.

Motion

There are a number of ways to show motion in a photograph and shutter speed is key. You can blur the motion with a slower shutter (1/60 sec and slower) or freeze the action with a higher speed such as 1/250 sec and faster. I recommend using a tripod (see chapter 12) for any shutter speed less than 1/30 sec (although it can't hurt at higher speeds, too!).

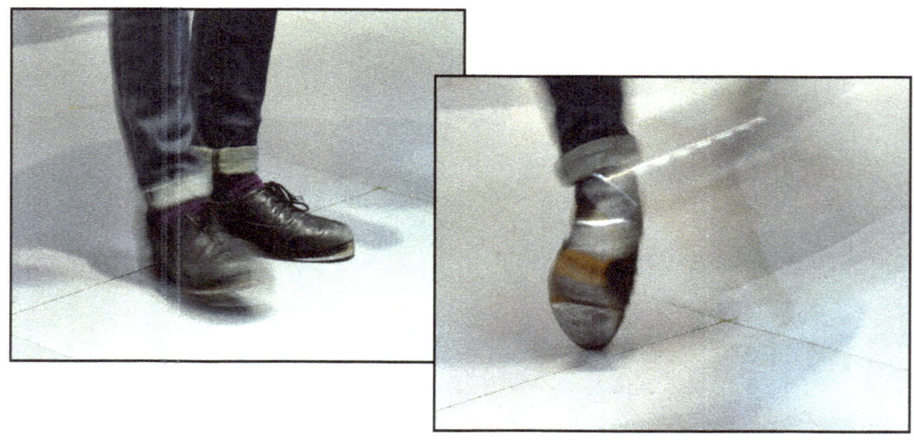

Tap dancing feet. Nikon D3200, shutter priority, center-weighted average, 1/15 sec, f/7.1, ISO 800, +0.3 EV, 55 mm, external flash, Philadelphia, PA.

In the first two images (previous page) of the tap dancing feet, the exposure is exactly the same, which means that the person was moving much faster in the right photograph because the right foot is completely blurred away, producing only a shadow. In the next two images below, the action is frozen thanks to a faster shutter speed of 1/200 sec.

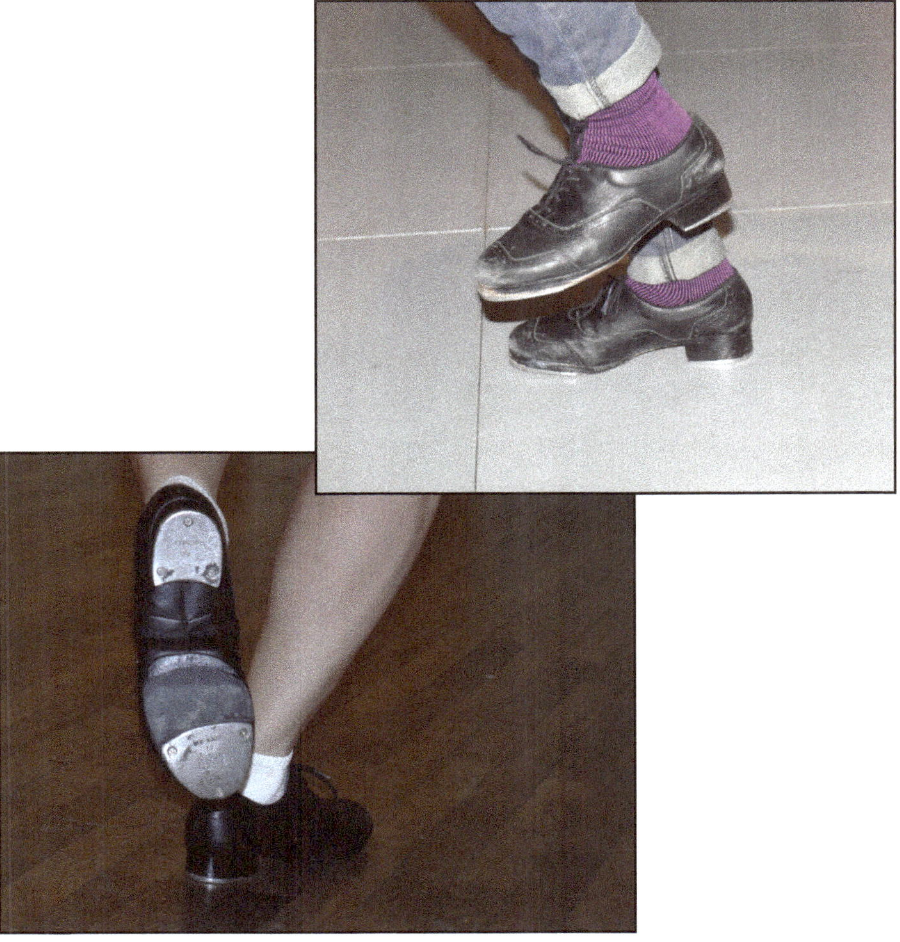

More tap dancing feet. Nikon D3200, shutter priority, center-weighted average, 1/200 sec, ISO 800, +0.3 EV, external flash, Philadelphia, PA. TOP: f/5, 51 mm. BOTTOM: f/5.6, 82 mm.

There's a technique called **panning** that blurs the background while keeping your moving subject fairly sharp. It requires a lot of practice to do well but the results are worth it! Panning works for subjects that are moving horizontally in front of you (rather than towards or away from you).

Follow your subject as it moves in front of you, keeping the camera focused on the subject as you go (you are moving your camera). In general, I push the shutter all the way down when the subject is just about in front of me. There are several keys to a good panning shot: keep your camera horizontal, choose a shutter speed that's fast enough to keep your subject clear but slow enough to blur the background, follow through on your own horizontal motion after you press the shutter button, and give your subject somewhere to go, so leave some room in front of it.

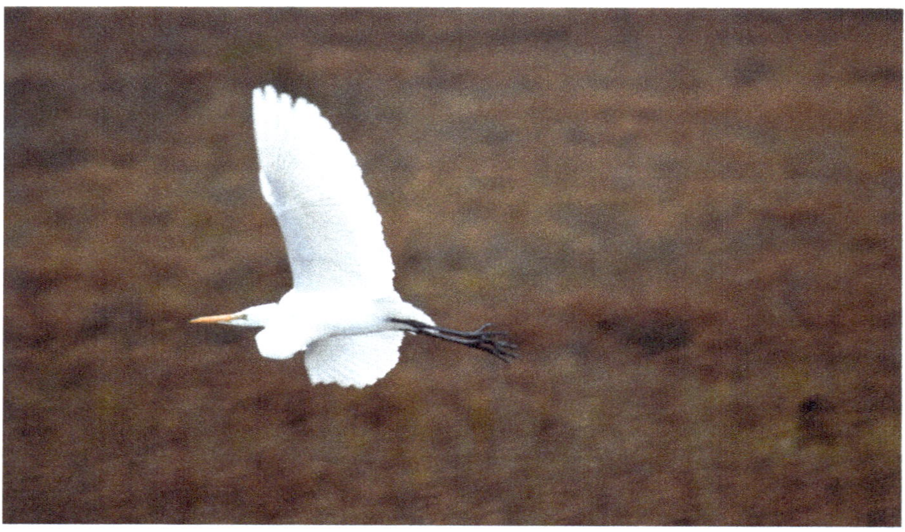

Great Egret. Nikon D3200, shutter priority, pattern metering, 1/200 sec, f/5.6, ISO 1600, 450 mm. Assateague Island, VA.

Running Horses. Minolta Maxxum 7D, aperture priority, pattern metering, 1/2 sec, f/6.3, ISO 400, 450 mm, +0.7 EV. Ocala, FL.

Burst (⧉) mode or continuous shooting mode is a way of showing motion through a series of images. As long as your finger is fully pressing the shutter button and the subject is in focus, the camera will record several shots per second (actual frames per second varies, depending on the camera). You do not need to be in shutter priority to shoot in burst mode.

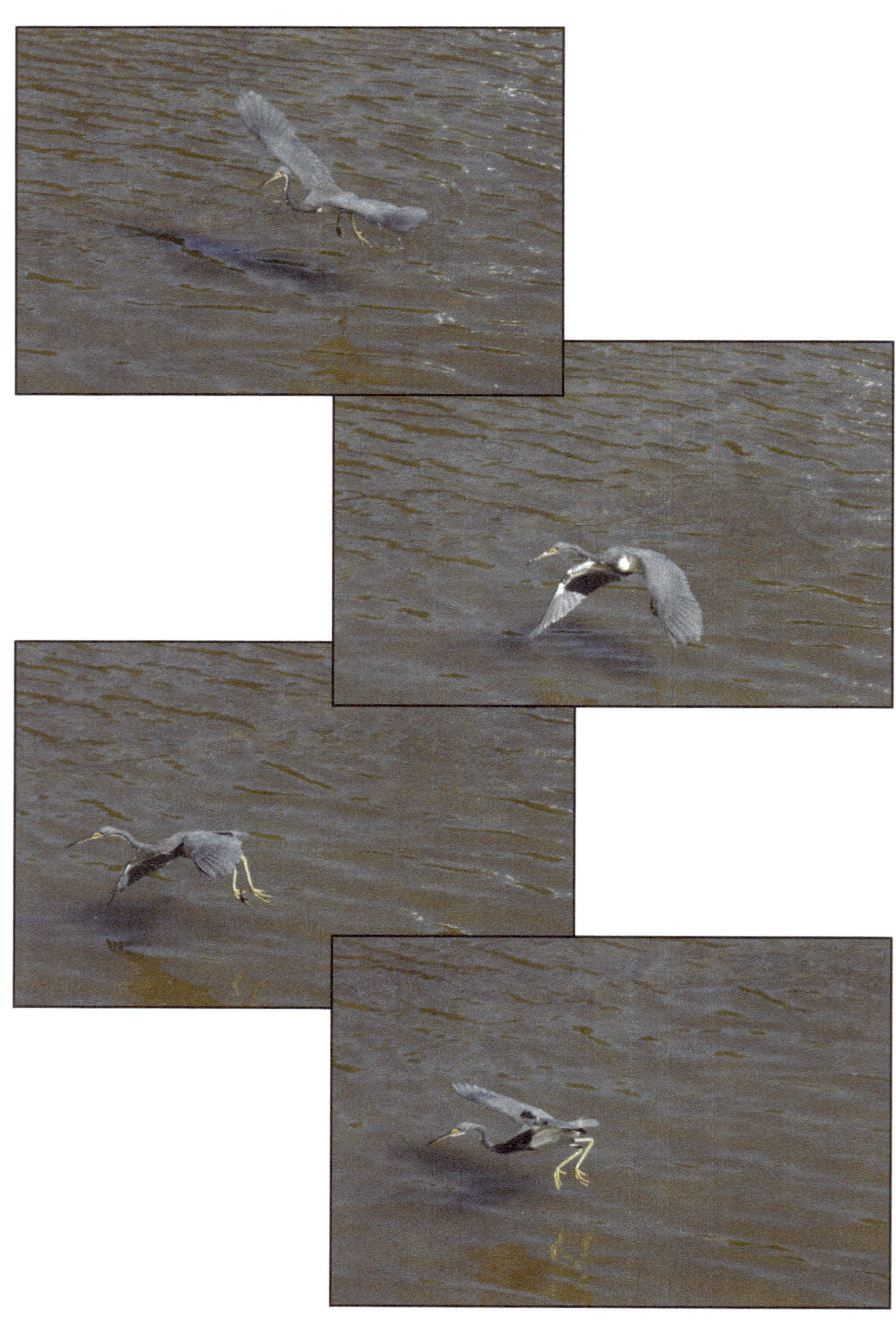

Great blue heron. Nikon D3200, shutter priority, center-weighted average, 1/640 sec, f/5.6, ISO 100, 202 mm, -0.7 EV. Sanibel Island, FL.

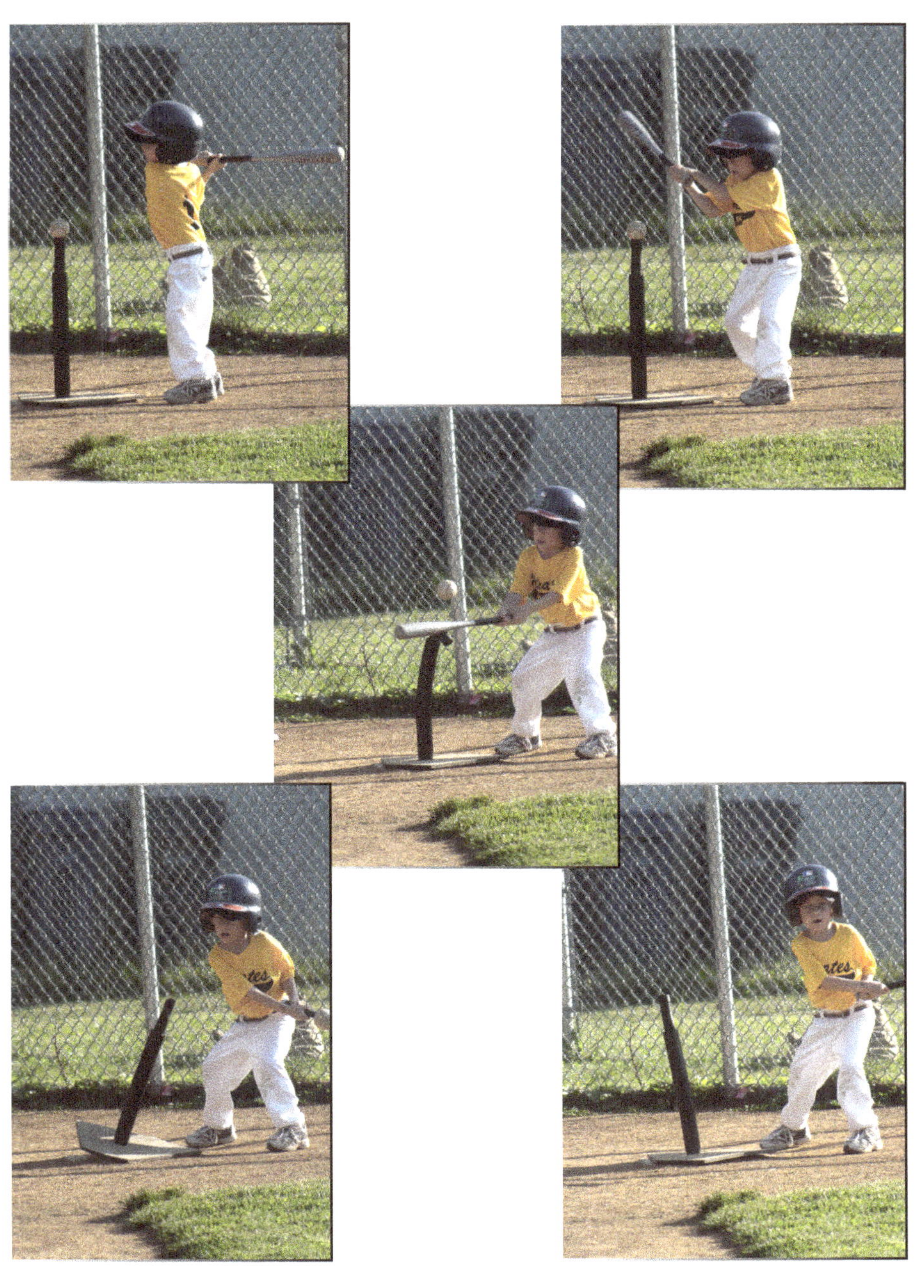

This is an example of "burst" mode in aperture priority (I was trying to blur as much of the background as possible with a wider aperture). T-ball. Sony A700, aperture priority, center-weighted metering, 1/400-1/500 sec, f/6.3, ISO 400, 420 mm. Glenside, PA.

Depth of Field (DOF)

Creating a sense of depth through focus falls in the realm of aperture. You don't need to be in aperture priority mode, but you do need to be aware of what your aperture is while you're taking pictures to understand the effect of different settings.

Let's compare these two photos of a feather on the sand. The first image has a narrower DOF – you can see the sand in the background gets blurry very quickly. The second image shows more detail in the sand, although it's not all in focus. The long telephoto lens helps to diminish the DOF, even at the smaller opening of f/22.

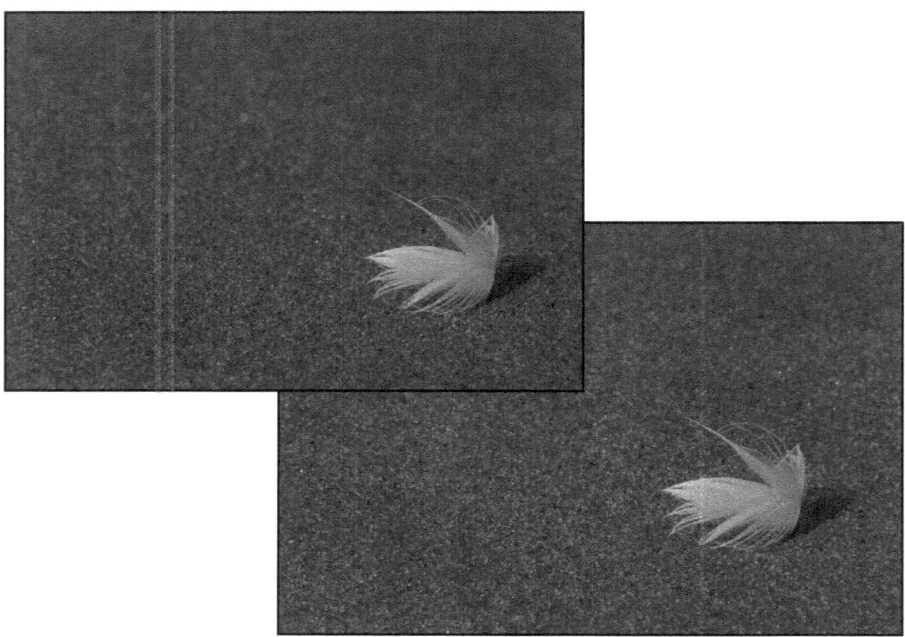

Minolta Maxxum 7D, shutter priority, pattern metering, ISO 200, -0.7 EV, 450 mm. TOP: 1/1000 sec, f/11. BOTTOM: 1/250 sec, f/22. Bombay Hook National Wildlife Refuge, DE.

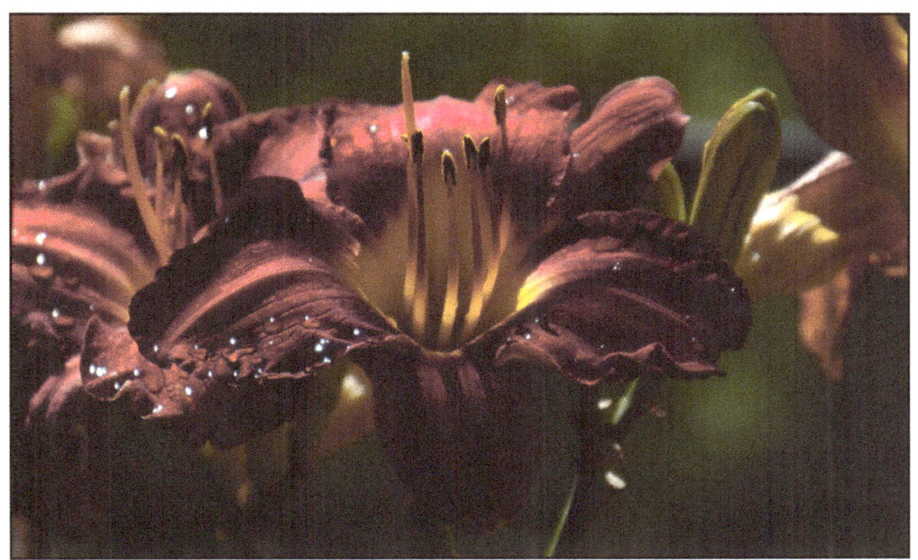

Notice the far side of the flower has a soft focus and the background is a green blur. 1/800 sec, f/6.3.

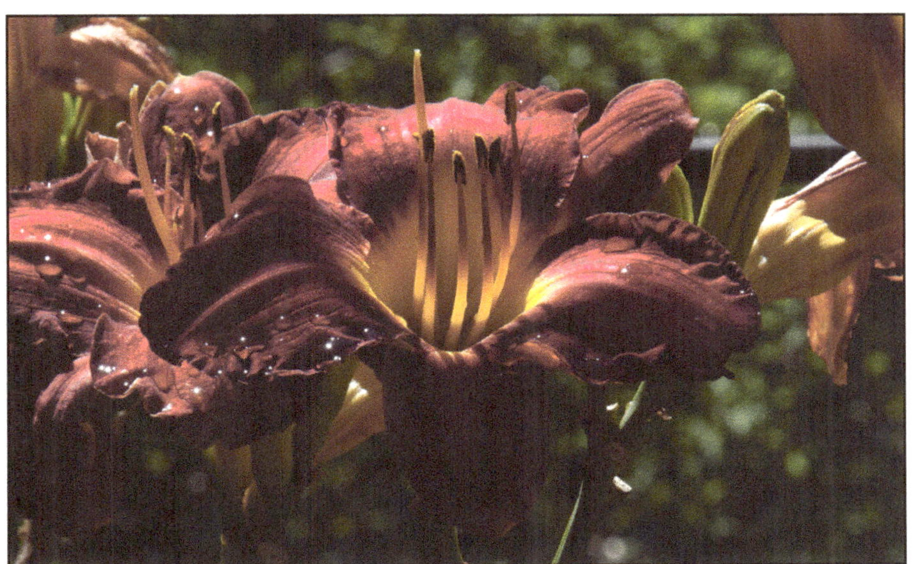

The back of the flower is pretty sharp but now the background is distracting. 1/50 sec, f/25.

Daylily. All images: Minolta Maxxum 7D, aperture priority, pattern metering, ISO 200, 270 mm. Morris Arboretum, Philadelphia, PA.

11.

Composition

What makes a good composition? While subjective, here are some guidelines to follow that will improve your chances of creating interesting and/or dynamic compositions.

Rule of thirds

Imagine a tic-tac-toe board that takes up the entire image. Instead of plopping your subject smack in the middle of the frame, put something of interest where two lines meet or along one of the horizontal or vertical lines.

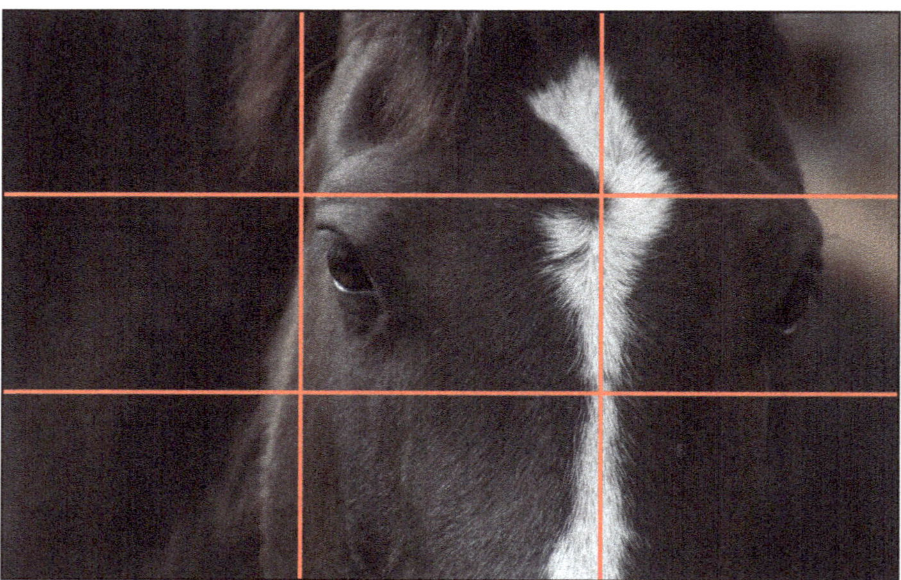

The white blaze is perfectly aligned with one vertical line and one eye is very close to two intersecting lines. Minolta Maxxum 7D, shutter priority, pattern metering, 1/640 sec, f/6.3, ISO 400, 450 mm, -0.7 EV.

Get closer

By either taking a few steps toward your subject or zooming in closer, you lessen the distractions of the background. Using a telephoto lens and large aperture (small f-stop number), you can further blur the background.

Photographing the entire tree is not a bad composition at all. But zooming in closer also makes for a nice image. Experiment!

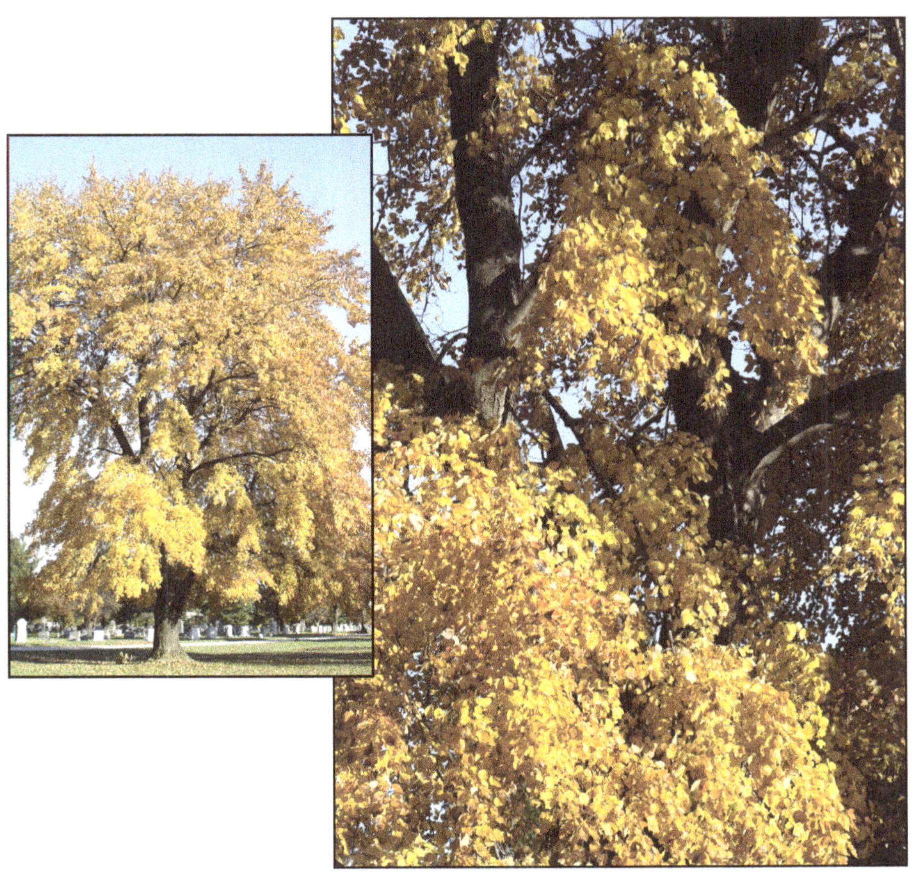

Both images: Minolta Maxxum 7D, shutter priority, spot metering, 1/200 sec, ISO 100. LEFT: f/5.6, 28 mm. RIGHT: f/8, 100 mm. Holy Sepulchre Cemetery, Philadelphia, PA.

Try a new perspective

Sometimes changing the height of the camera, angle of view, or turning the camera vertical can make a huge difference between a boring snapshot and an exciting image.

Instead of shooting the horse and rider with their reflection, I honed in on the reflection only, providing an interesting perspective on the scene.

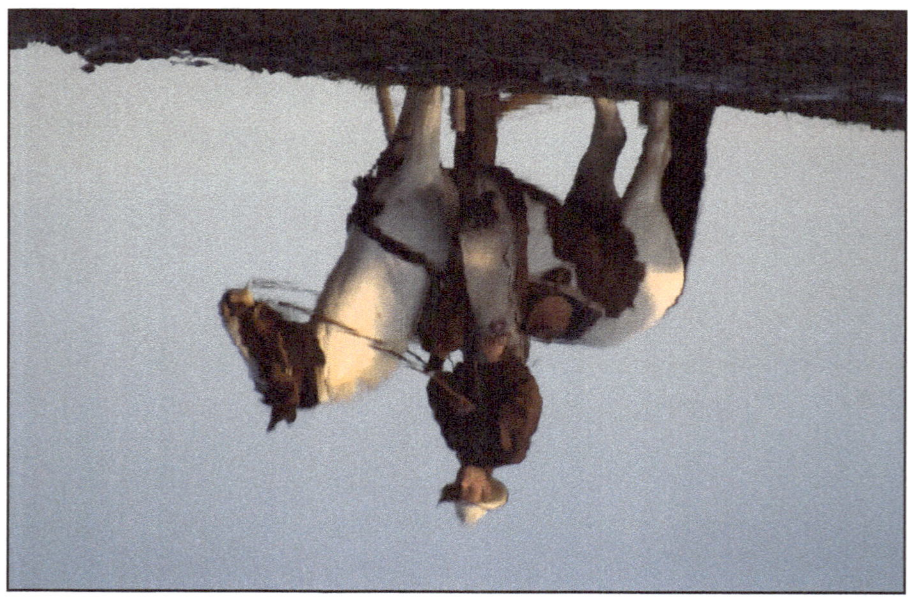

Minolta Maxxum 7D, shutter priority, spot metering, 1/250 sec, f/6.3, ISO 400, 345 mm, -0.7 EV. Craig, CO.

Put the eye in the middle

When photographing a person or animal, try to place the subject's eye in the middle of the frame and focus on that point.

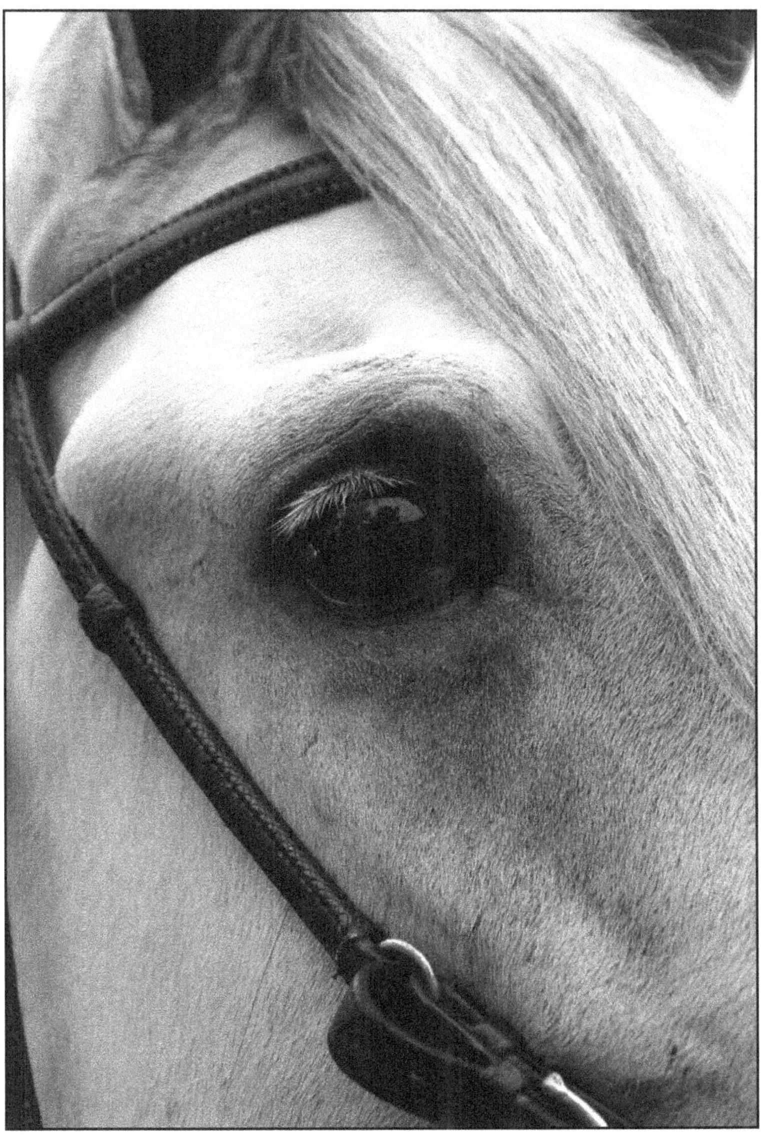

Minolta Maxxum 7D, shutter priority, pattern metering, 1/500 sec, f/8, ISO 800, 450 mm, +0.5 EV. Ocala, FL.

Diagonals

Create some interest by using diagonals that lead you into and around the image.

I found the lines of and in the roof very interesting. There are lots of diagonals here!

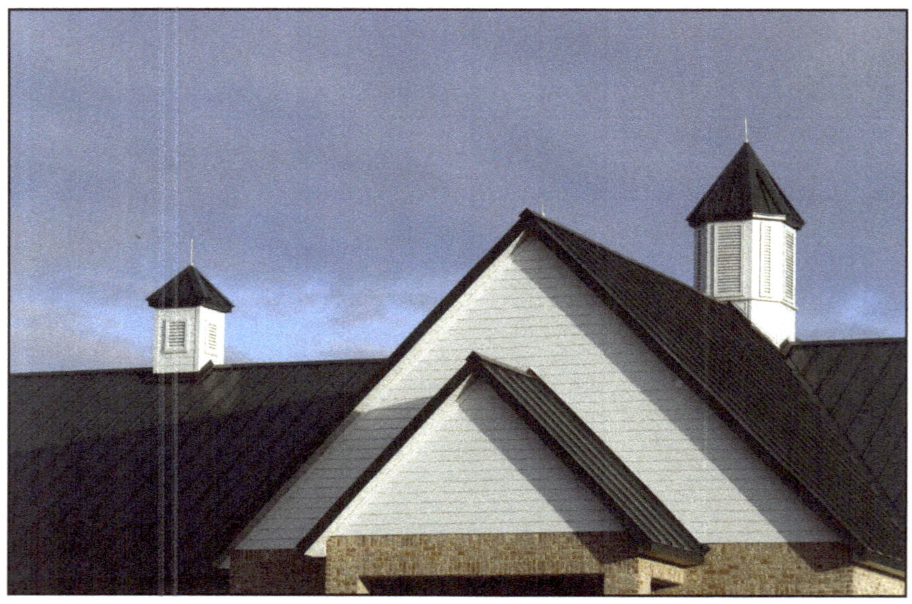

Minolta Maxxum 7D, shutter priority, pattern metering, 1/1000 sec, f/11, ISO 400, 127 mm, -0.3 EV. Ocala, FL.

Leading lines

Lines and roads can give a viewer a way into an image and then roam around, noticing other details.

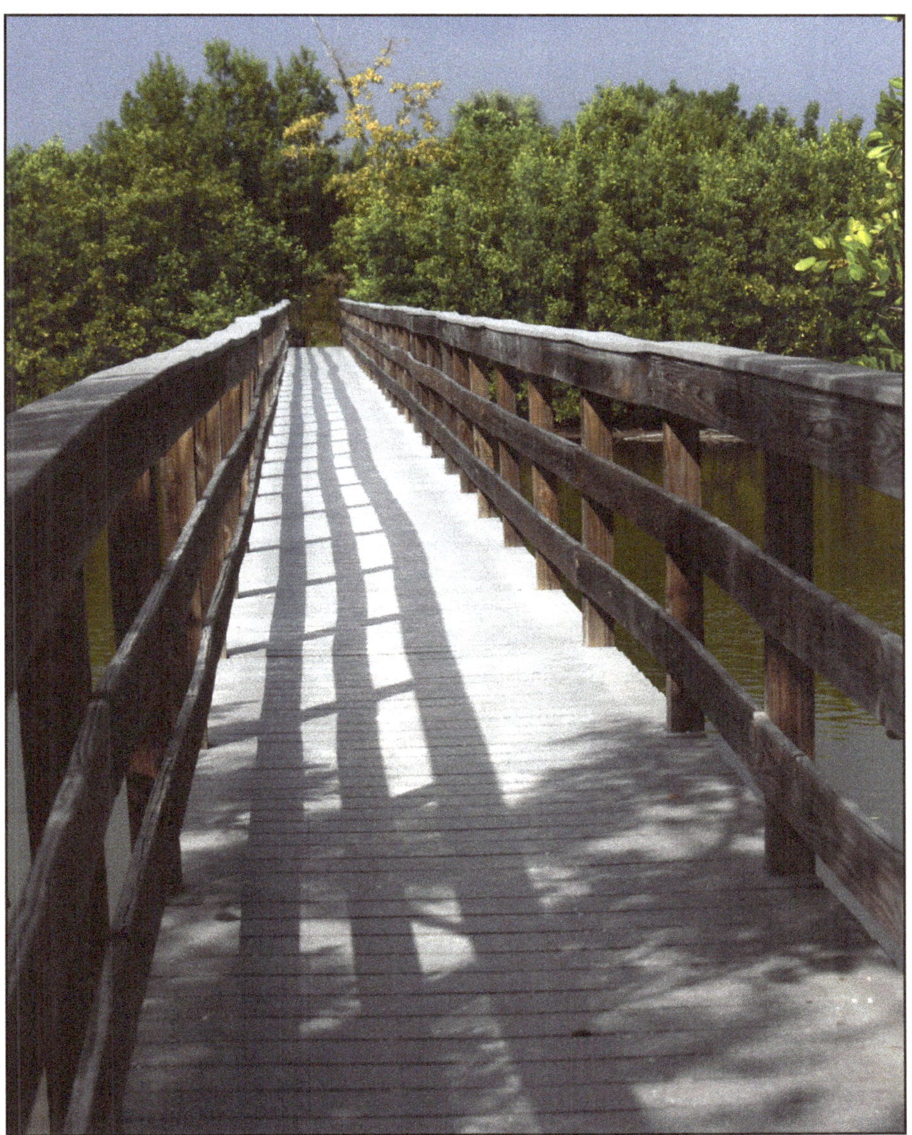

Sony A700, shutter priority, center-weighted metering, 1/1250 sec, f/9, ISO 200, 75 mm, -1.3 EV. Sanibel Island, FL.

Patterns

Many people are attracted to repeating patterns. Look for these as you're exploring: bricks, stones, roofing materials, windows, etc.

I took several pictures of this expansive brick sidewalk/patio area. Just keep shooting; you never know which shot will be THE ONE.

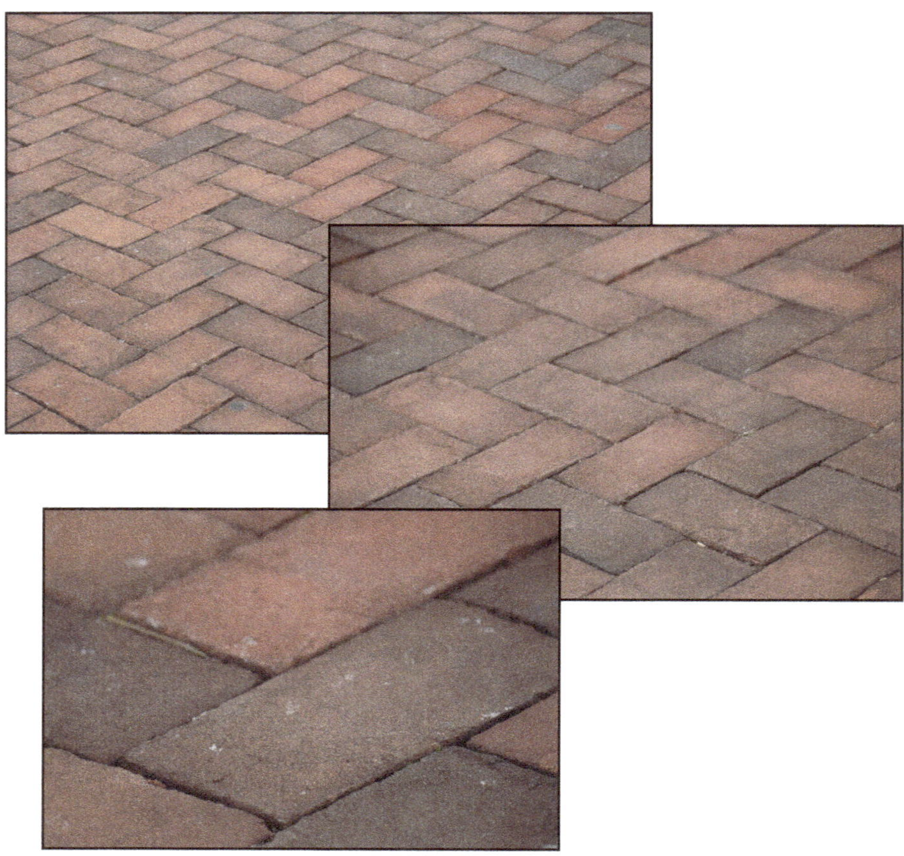

All images: Nikon D3200, aperture priority, matrix metering, ISO 100, -0.3 EV. TOP: 1/80 sec, f/4.5, 82 mm. MIDDLE: 1/60 sec, f/4.8, 153 mm. BOTTOM: 1/50 sec, f/5.6, 450 mm. Fairmount Waterworks, Philadelphia, PA.

80

Selective focus

Using a narrow depth of field will leave a relatively small area in sharp focus and the rest of the image will be more blurry. Your viewer's eye will go straight to what's in focus, so make sure that's your intended subject.

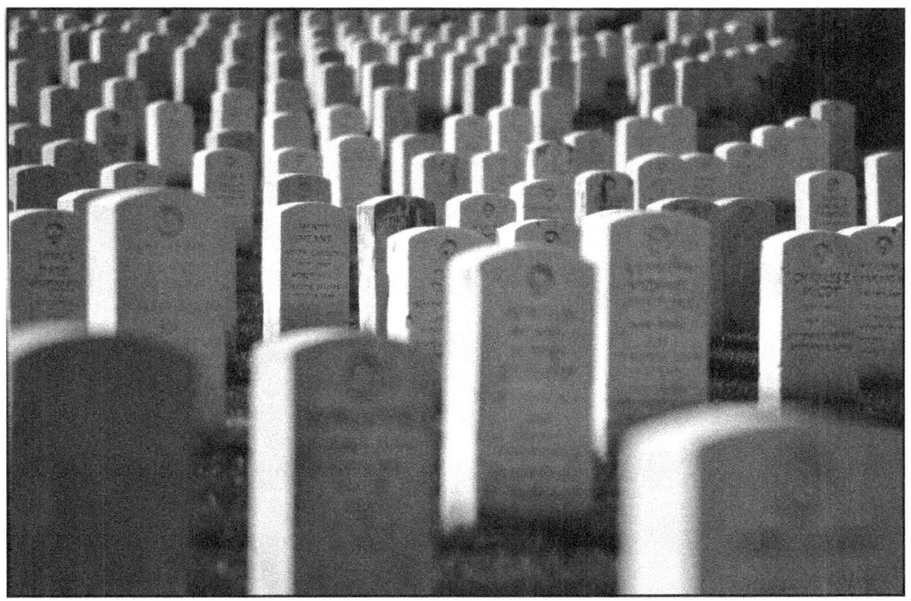

Nikon D3200, aperture priority, center-weighted metering, 1/4000 sec, f/5.6, ISO 400, 450 mm, -0.3 EV. Arlington National Cemetery, Arlington, VA.

Framing

Use a doorway, window, trees, or other objects on the sides, bottom, or top to frame your subject.

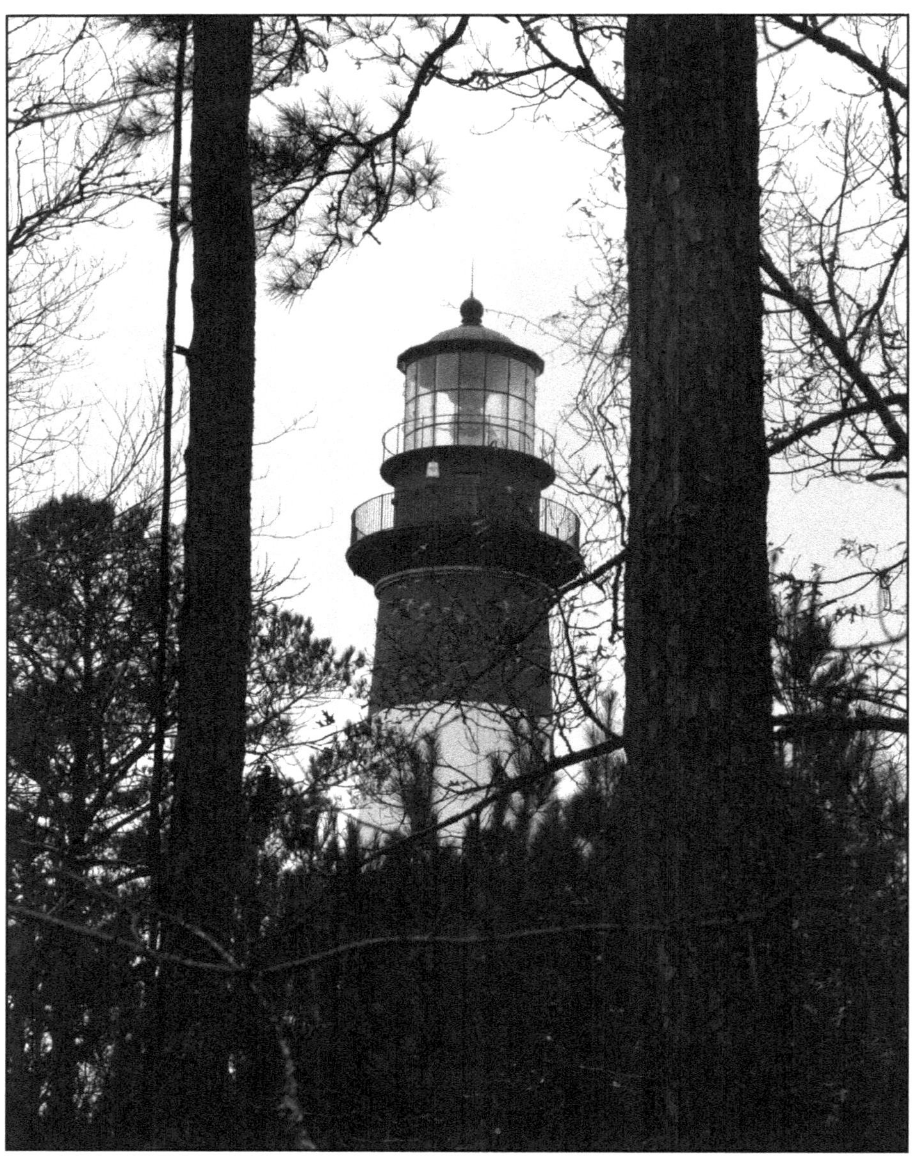

Nikon D3200, shutter priority, pattern metering, 1/200 sec, f/14, ISO 1600, 120 mm. Assateague Island, VA.

Try something different!

Sometimes you just need to experiment in weird ways: move the camera while you're pressing the shutter; focus manually; use the "wrong" white balance. The choice is yours.

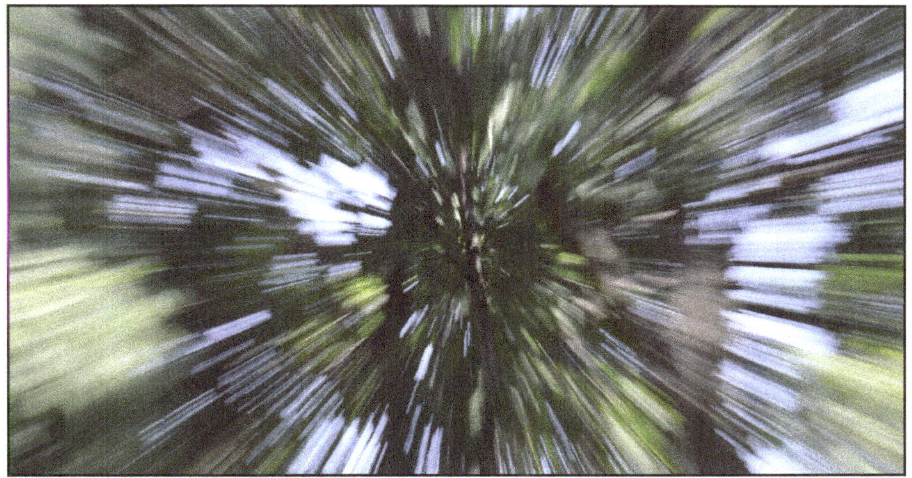

I moved the zoom while I pressed the shutter button. Nikon D3200, shutter priority, pattern metering, 1/5 sec, f/22, ISO 100, 127 mm.

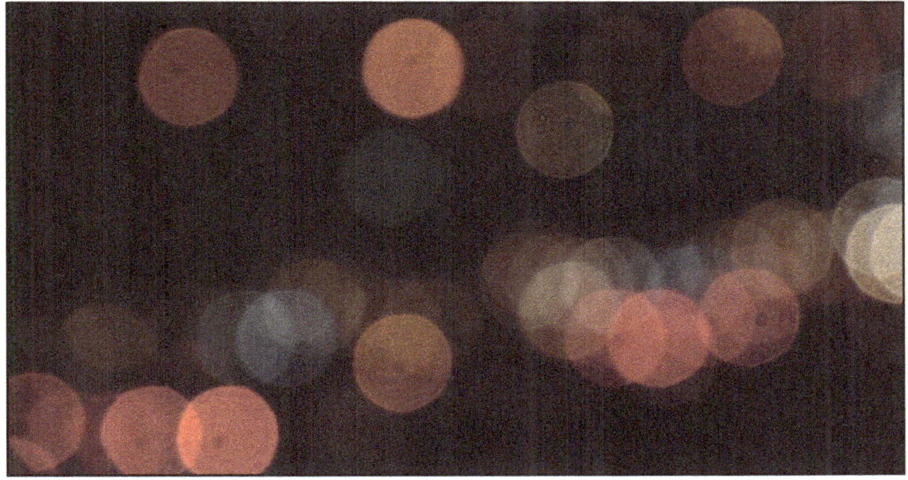

I intentionally shot these lights (head and tail lights from cars on a nearby highway) out of focus. Nikon D7000, manual, spot metering, 1/13 sec, f/8, ISO 100, 450 mm. Philadelphia, PA.

Be aware of backgrounds

Sometimes in the rush to get the shot, we don't realize there's something odd in the background that negatively affects the image. Here, it's the bubbles on the water below the icicles (bottom photo). By timing it right, I was able to eliminate that distraction.

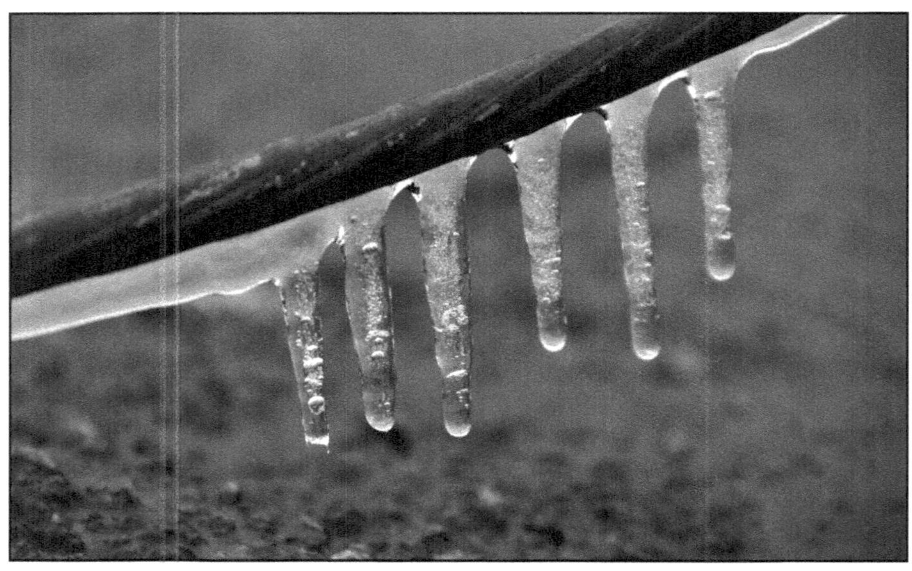

Nikon D7000, manual, spot metering, f/7.1, ISO 320, 450 mm.
TOP: 1/400 sec. BOTTOM: 1/320 sec. Conowingo Dam, MD.

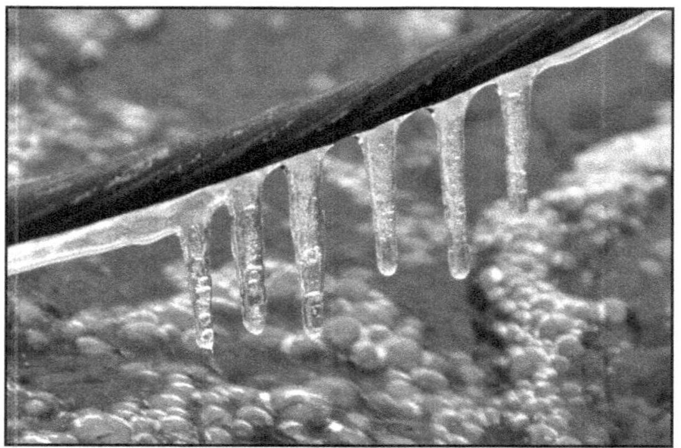

12.
Extras

Tripod/Monopod

A tripod is one of the best investments you can make in your photography equipment. Even with vibration reduction built into your camera and/or lens, there's nothing like a tripod to ensure that your camera doesn't move when you take a picture. When you're shooting at slow shutter speeds, a steady, sturdy hold is required. A tripod fits that bill very well. Using a tripod also makes it easier to change camera settings so you can try various apertures, shutter speeds, white balance, or ISO settings without changing your composition.

A monopod has just one leg, your legs complete the tri. It's still possible to move the camera when you're using a monopod but there's less to carry and with practice, you can increase your steadiness.

When you're ready to buy a tripod or monopod, there are several attributes to consider: type of head (ball, pan/tilt, pistol grip, gimbal), leg locks (levers or twist), tallest height, lowest working height, and weight. Regardless of what you choose, make sure the tripod and head can support the weight of the gear you have (or plan to purchase).

Here's the low down on some of the pros and cons of each.

Head: This is a removable piece that attaches your camera to the tripod or monopod.

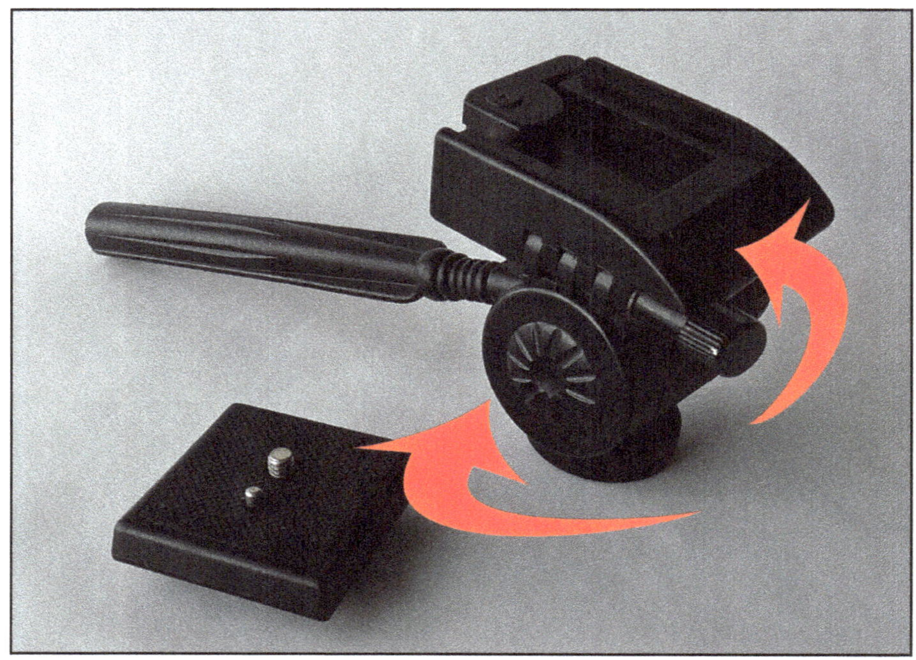

Pan/tilt head (above): You're basically working in two dimensions- left/right and horizontal to vertical on various angles. There's no maneuverability in other directions.

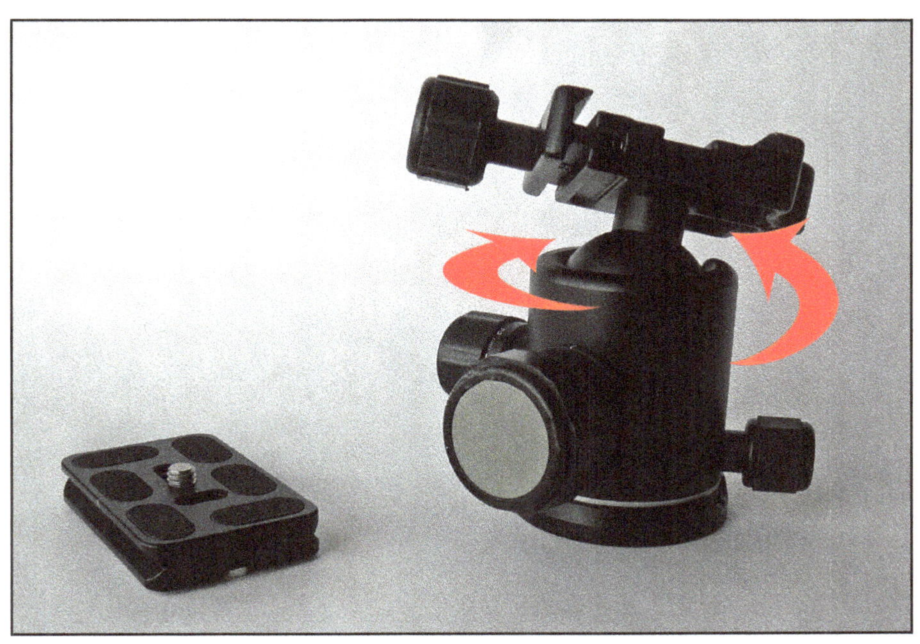

Ball head (above): You can adjust in all directions/angles.

Pistol grip and *gimbal* heads (not pictured) are both based on the ball idea. The pistol grip adjusts position by squeezing the grip to loosen and move it; letting go will lock it. A gimbal head attaches to long, heavy lenses, rather than the camera body. Position adjustments are made like a ball head.

Leg Locks: How you adjust the height of the monopod or tripod.

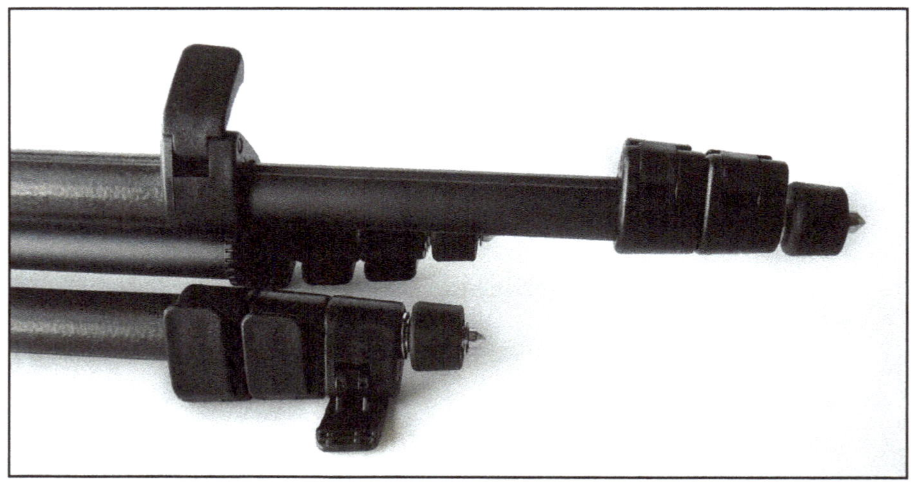

Levers: Quick move to unlock the section.

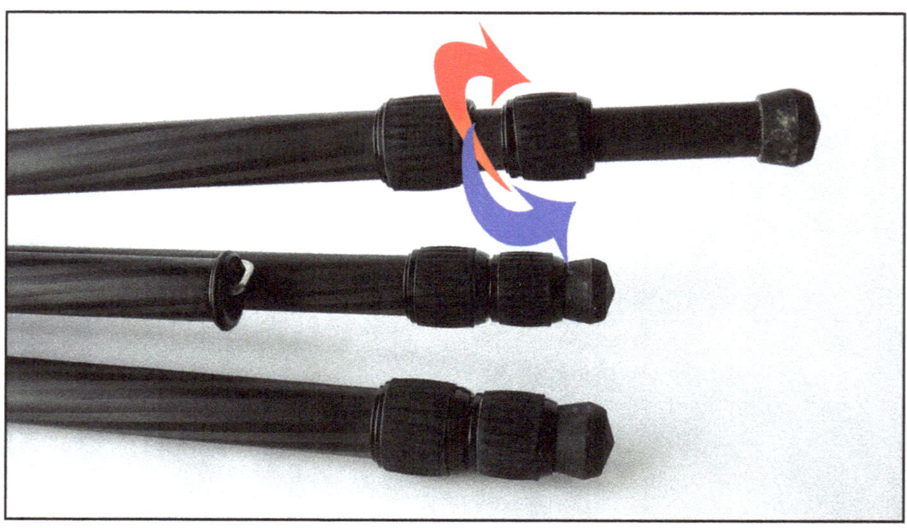

Twist: Like a screw, twist one way to loosen; twist the other way to tighten. You can loosen several sections at once to make setting up and taking down faster.

Tallest Height: How high would you like your tripod/monopod to go? If you're tall, you'll want a taller tripod so you're not always bending over to look through your camera. The camera will become less steady if you rely on raising the central column rather than getting a tripod with longer legs.

Lowest Working Height: If you do a lot of work close to the ground, you'll want a tripod that can also get low to the ground with different leg angles and/or a short central column.

Once you have decided on the above features, you can choose any two of the following three: sturdy, light, or inexpensive. You can't have all three. If you choose sturdy and light, it will be expensive. If you choose light and inexpensive, it won't be sturdy. Sturdy and inexpensive won't be light. If you're going to invest in a tripod, make sure it's sturdy. If you need it to be light because you like to hike with your camera, be prepared to pay more.

Filters

Filters screw onto the end of your lens and can stay there at all times or attached only when needed. Here are a few that you might want to consider adding to your camera bag. You'll need to know the filter size of your lens(es) so that you buy the correct size. If you have more than one lens and each is a different size, you'll need to buy multiple filters or filter adapter(s) to use one filter on more than one lens.

Skylight or UV: This is a filter you can leave on the front of your lens all the time as protection from dust, scratches, and smudges. If the filter is damaged in any way, it's a lot less expensive than replacing the lens. There's some disagreement in the photography community as to whether this filter is truly necessary. There are concerns about loss of image quality from using a cheaper filter or how much dust, smears, and scratches affect the lens or filter. I leave a UV filter on each of my lenses.

Circular Polarizer: A polarizing filter helps to block the sun at certain angles. This can help reduce reflections on glass and water surfaces. It can also darken the blue of the sky and cut through some haze. Once attached to your lens, the filter rotates so you can adjust the angle of the light to filter. Keep in mind that when you use this filter, it blocks some of the incoming light which will require adjusting your exposure.

Clouds. Nikon D3200, shutter priority, center-weighted metering, 1/500 sec, ISO 200, 120 mm. TOP: without polarizer, f/9. BOTTOM: with polarizer, f/7.1 (sky is bluer, clouds are more apparent). Beaufort, NC.

Notice the difference between the reflections in the water below. Sometimes the reflection is what you want and other times you may want to avoid them.

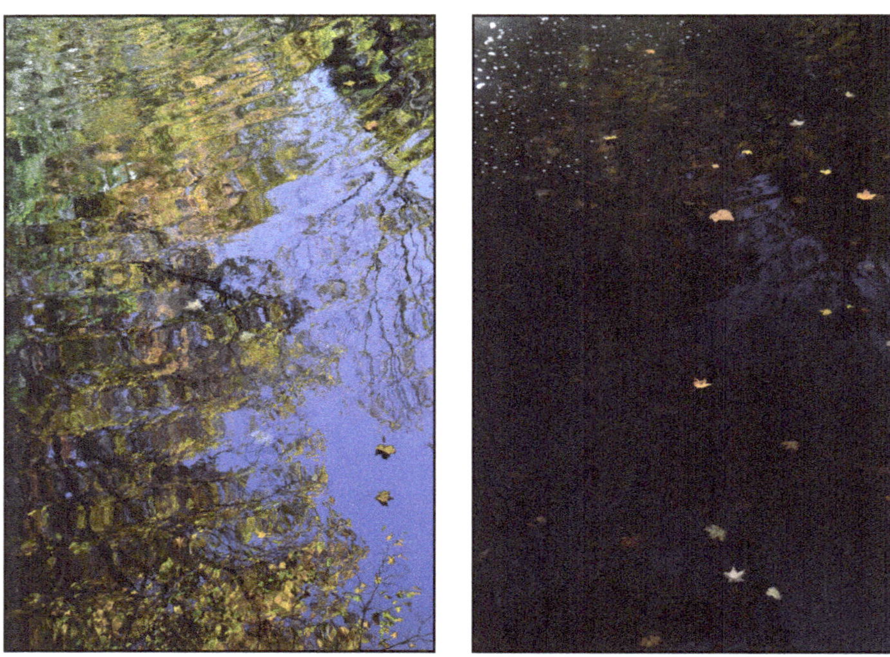

Reflections in water. Nikon D7000, manual, pattern metering, 1/50 sec, f/5, ISO 400, 87 mm. LEFT: without polarizer. RIGHT: with polarizer.

Neutral Density (ND): These don't affect the color of the scene, but reduce the amount of light coming through the lens. They come in different strengths, such as +1, +2, +5 and can be combined to create darker filters. There are other filters that are variable: they go from +1 to +5 (or other strengths) by rotating the filter once it's attached. Neutral density filters are handy to have when you want to use slower shutter speeds.

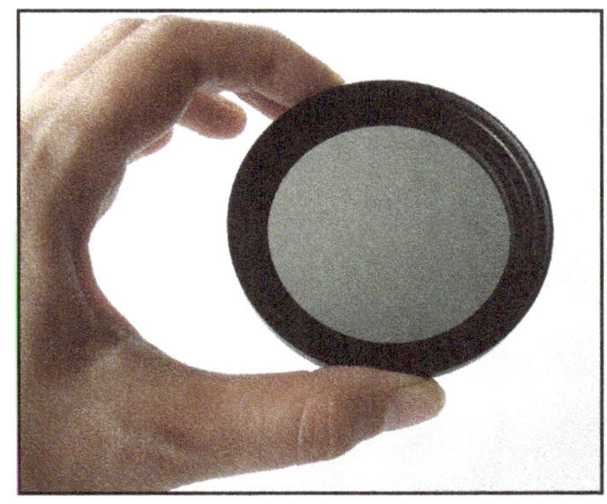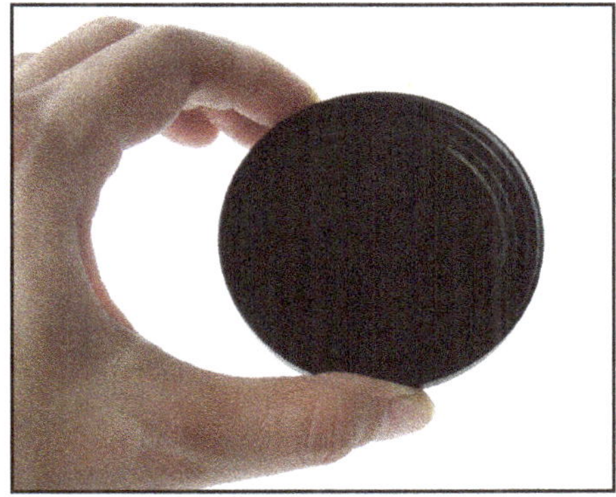

Variable Neutral Density filter. LEFT: lower density. RIGHT: higher density.

Without a neutral density filter, it would be impossible to use a shutter speed of 1 or more seconds in bright sun and keep detail in the water (it would be pure white), see examples, below and the following page.

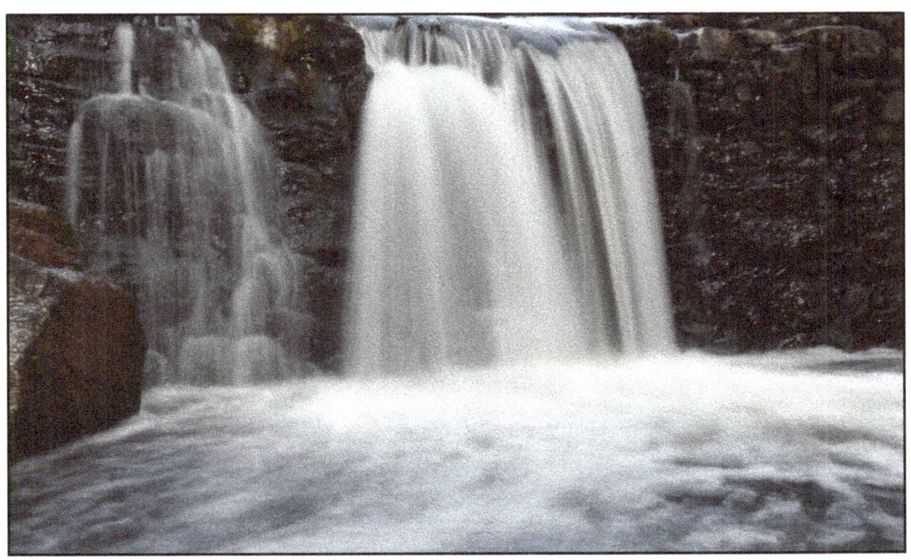

Nikon D7000, aperture priority, pattern metering, 0.77 sec, f/25, ISO 250, 75 mm with a variable ND filter. Wissahickon Valley, Philadelphia, PA.

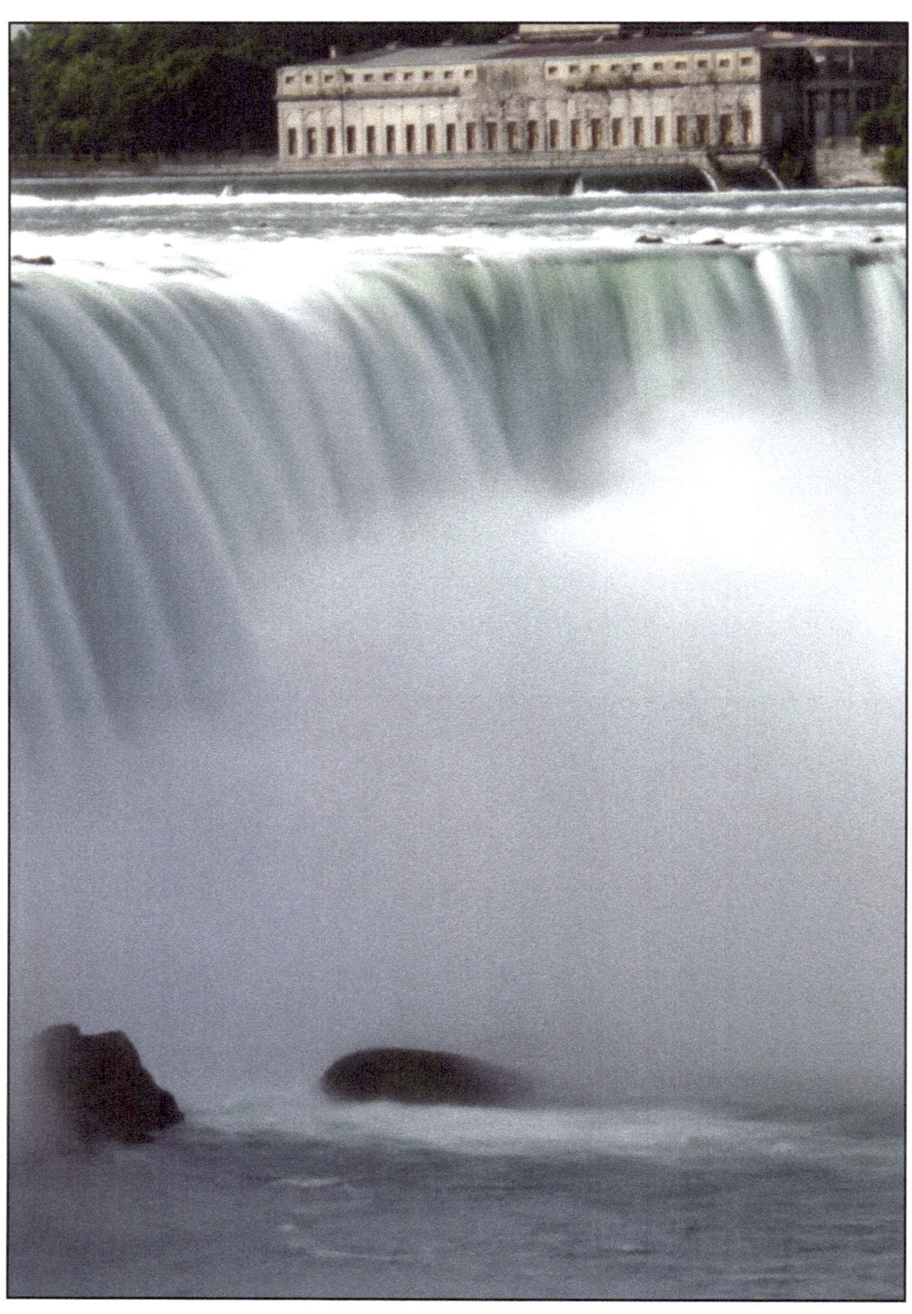

Horseshoe Falls. Nikon D3200, shutter priority, center-weighted metering, 1.3 sec, f/36, ISO 100, 98 mm, with variable ND filter. Niagara Falls, Canada.

There are also graduated filters (not illustrated) which go from clear to darker across a portion of the filter. These are ideal for darkening the sky without affecting the rest of the scene such as sunrise, sunset, or a canyon/valley in shadow.

Close-up: It's like attaching a macro lens but for a much lower price. These filters drastically reduce the focusing distance needed between the end of the lens and the subject. However, finding the sweet spot from where to focus will take some practice (knowing how far from the subject to set your camera/tripod).

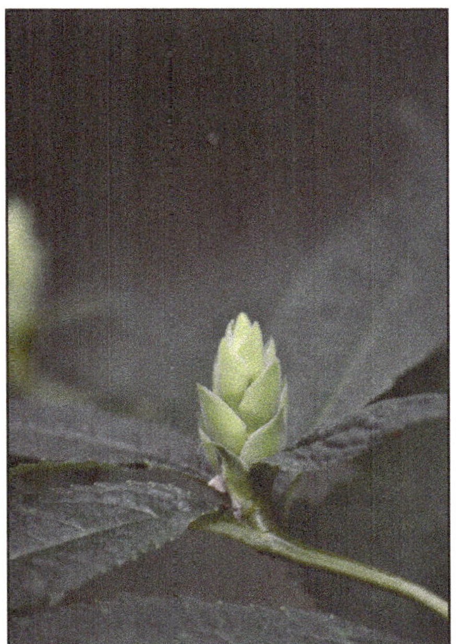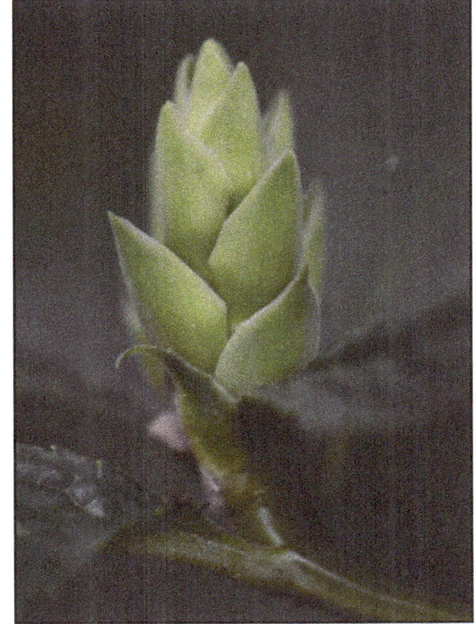

Nikon D3200, aperture priority, pattern metering, f/5.6, ISO 250. LEFT: without close-up filter, 1/50 sec, 450 mm. RIGHT: with close-up filter, 1/100 sec, 390 mm.

13.

Flash

Your camera comes with a built-in flash that may not be very powerful, but it can be useful. Keep in mind that most cameras set a maximum shutter speed (1/200 sec is common) when using the flash. Without that restriction, your image could be only partially exposed with a faster shutter speed (the shutter closes before the light from the flash has fully illuminated your subject). Even with that upper limit, using the flash at 1/200 second often succeeds in freezing any action.

Fill flash outdoors

When you're in the shade, there may not be enough light to use the shutter speed or aperture that you would like unless you use the flash.

On the next page is an example of a little toad I encountered while walking in the woods (I was surprised it didn't hop away). The first image is without the flash and a good distance away. It's circled in red because otherwise you may have a hard time spotting it in the dark photo. I took another photo using the flash, and a third photo where I got pretty close and used the flash to finally get a decent image. Using the flash does change the quality of the light so the last photo doesn't look natural, in my opinion.

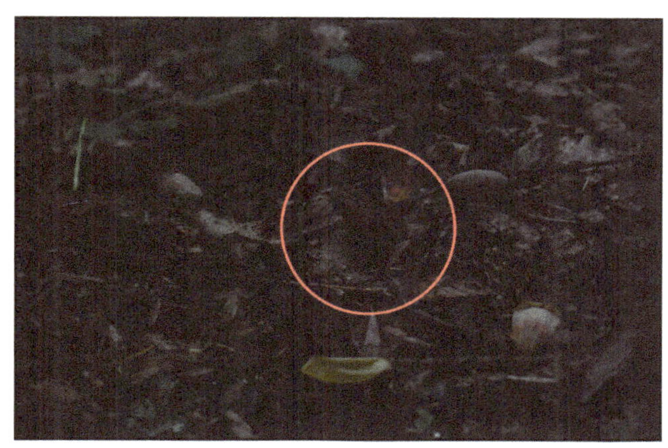

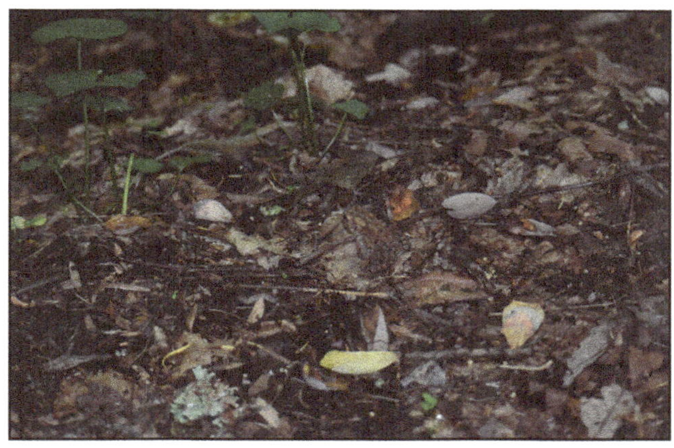

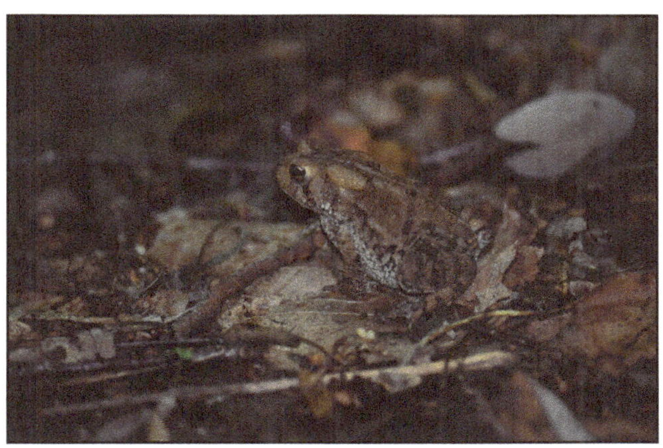

TOP: 1/250 sec, f/4.5, 105 mm. MIDDLE: 1/250 sec, f/4.5, 82 mm, flash. BOTTOM: 1/250 sec, f/5, 277 mm, flash.

All images: Nikon D7000, shutter priority, pattern metering, ISO 1000, +0.3 EV. Pequea, PA.

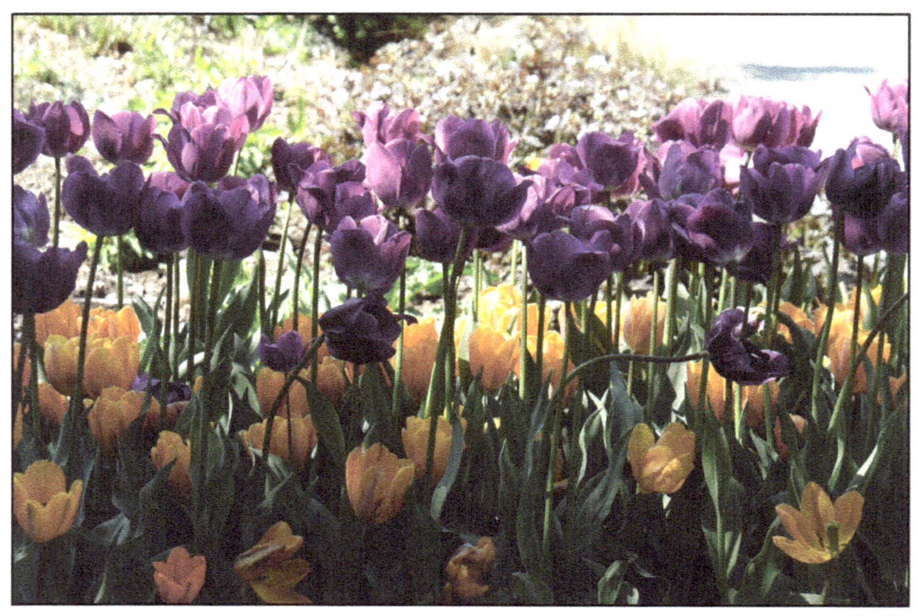

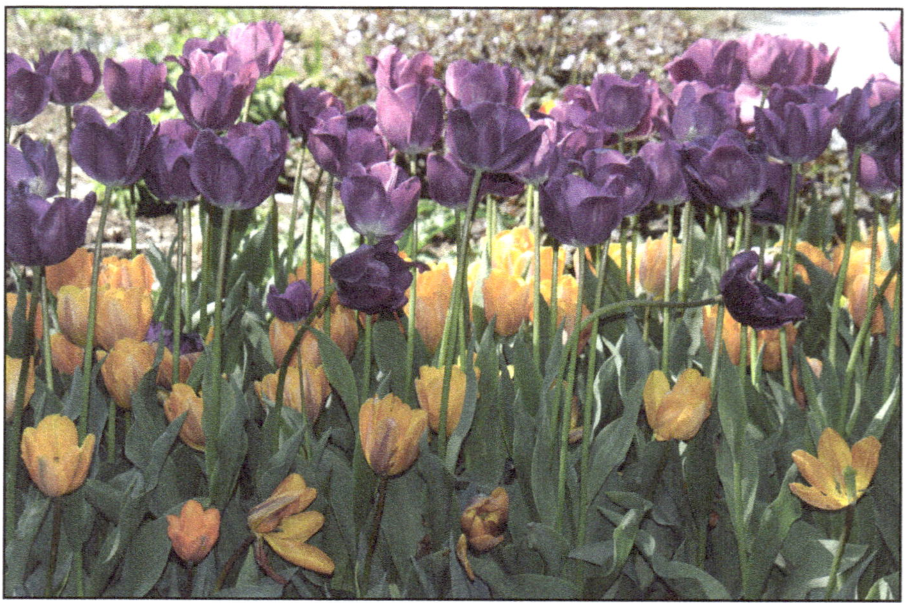

Tulips. Sony A700, aperture priority, pattern metering, f/7.1, ISO 200, 105 mm. TOP: 1/160 sec, no flash. BOTTOM: 1/200 sec, with fill flash. Morris Arboretum, Philadelphia, PA.

Flash indoors

Using your built-in flash indoors is useful in a pinch. But beware of the harsh shadows it can create behind your subject(s). If you find that you take a lot of indoor photos and need a flash, consider investing in one that you can attach to the hotshoe above the viewfinder. External flash units that can be angled when the camera is horizontal and vertical will give you the most options (but also cost more).

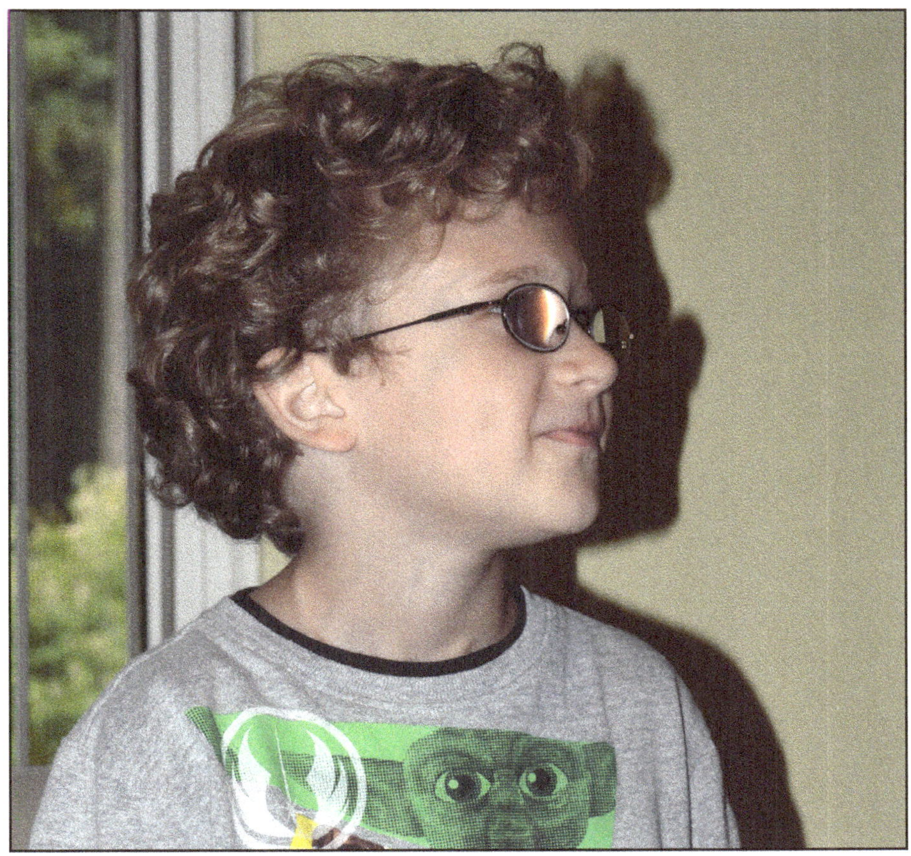

Nikon D3200, shutter priority, pattern metering, 1/100 sec, f/5.3, ISO 400, 63 mm, with built-in flash.

The following images of a bowl of fruit show some of the flash options available: auto without flash, auto with flash, and an external flash that can bounce the light off the ceiling first to reduce shadows behind the subject.

In this case, auto without the flash or the external flash that was aimed at an angle toward the ceiling are good options. Adjusting the angle of the external flash requires some trial and error to get the best result. That's easy to do with a bowl of stationary fruit; it's harder when photographing moving people at an event.

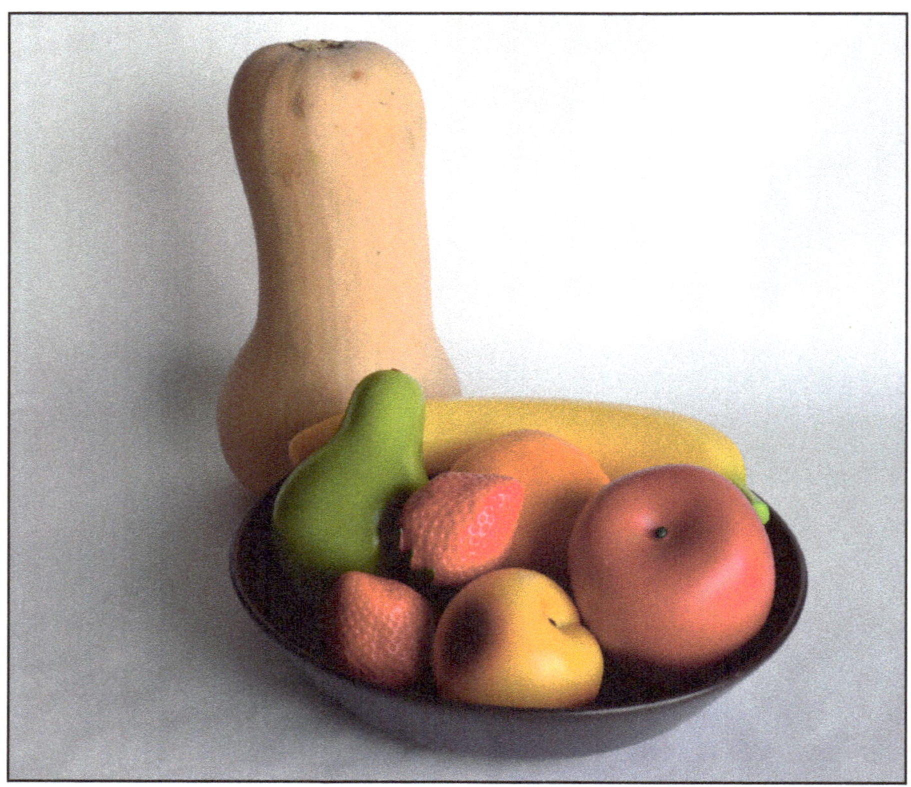

Auto, without flash. Shadow is to the left/behind the objects due to the natural lighting from a window to the right. 1/80 sec, f/4.5.

100

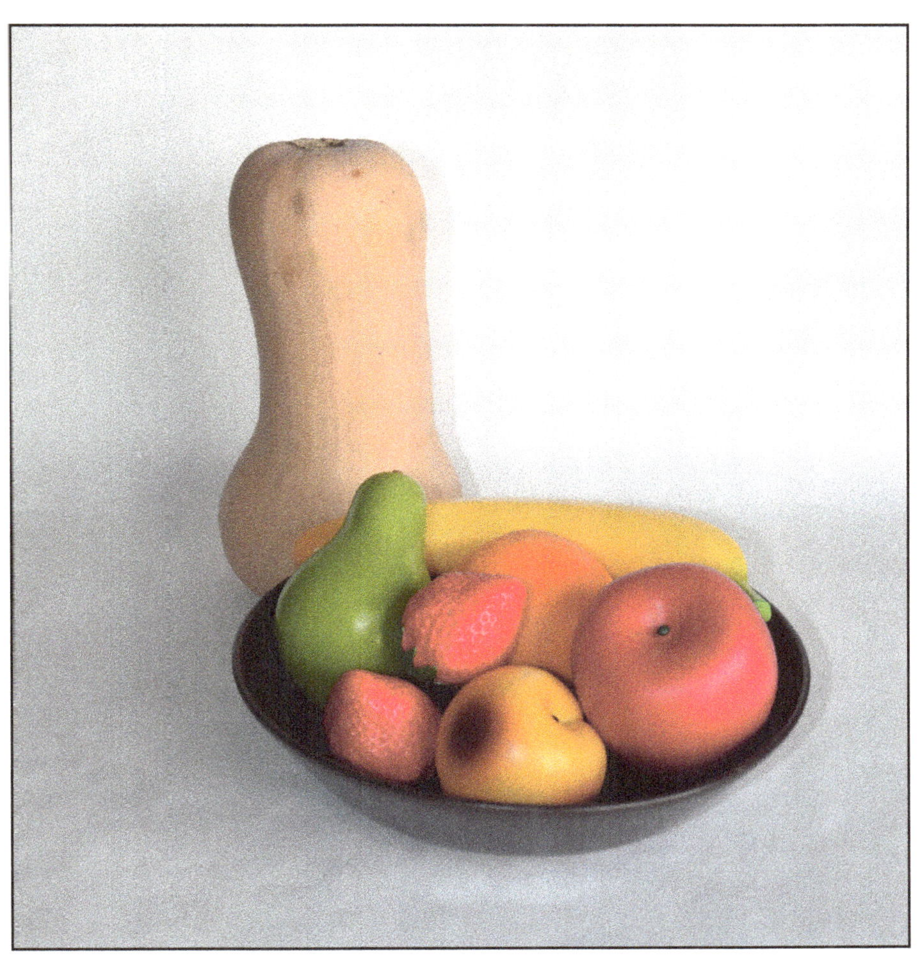

Auto, with flash. Shadow visible to the right/behind the squash and bowl edge. 1/80 sec, f/4.5.

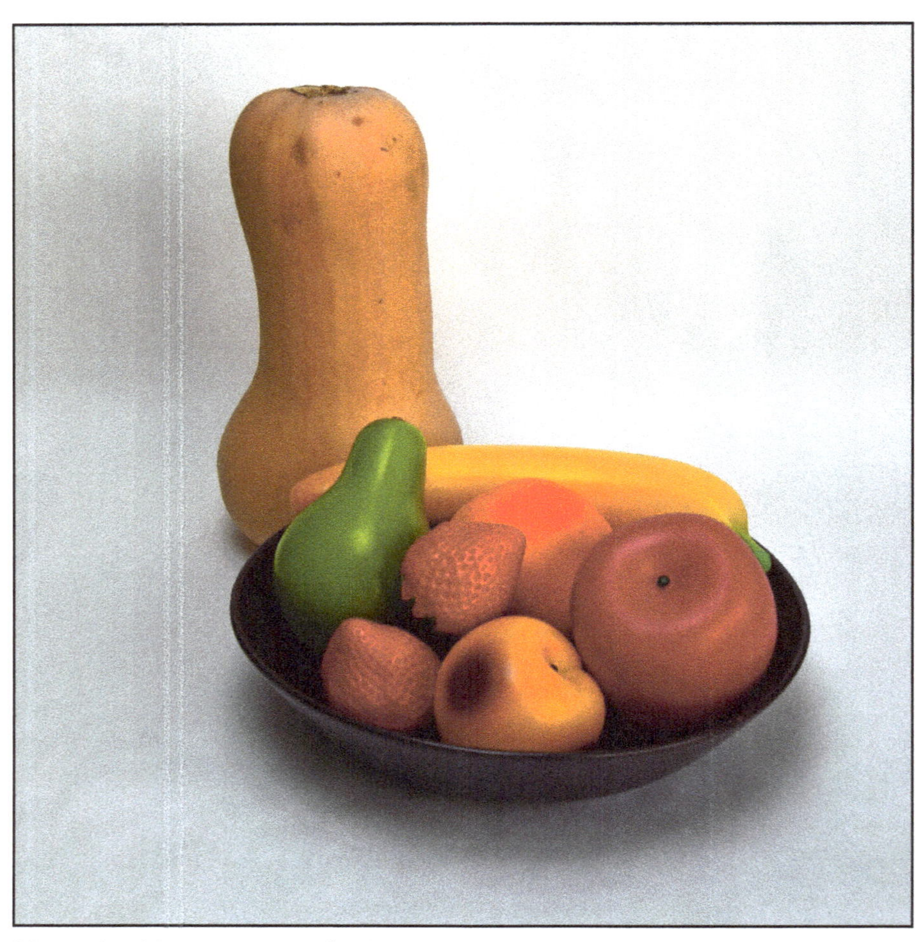

Manual, with an external flash, aimed at an angle toward the ceiling. The shadow is under the bowl. 1/60 sec, f/7.1.

14.

Printing

How do you determine the number of pixels needed for the print size you want? We'll need to do some math...and it involves the number of pixels you have and the resolution required to make a print. The rule of thumb has always been that you need a resolution of 300 pixels/inch (ppi) to get a decent print. This is still true for professionally printed pictures (such as a photo lab and for books or magazines). It's not necessarily true for inkjet printers which need at least 150 ppi to make very good prints; although higher ppi will produce better and/or larger prints.

Let's start with the number of pixels you have, such as 3000 x 4512 (13.5 MP). If you want a print that's 10 in x 15 in, divide your pixels by the corresponding size you want, to get the resolution:

pixels / print height (or width) = resolution

In this case, 3000 pixels / 10 inches = 300 ppi. And 4512 pixels / 15 inches = 300.8 ppi. That's perfect for a print from a lab on photo paper. If you wanted a print that was 20 in x 30 in: 3000 pixels / 20 inches = 150 ppi and 4512 pixels / 30 inches = 150.4 ppi. That should be fine for an inkjet print.

You could also calculate the number of pixels needed by multiplying the dimensions you want by the resolution.

print height (or width) x resolution = pixels

Let's say you'd like a print that's 16 in x 20 in. For math that's relatively easy, choose a resolution of 200 ppi: 16 in x 200 ppi = 3200 pixels and 20 in x 200 ppi = 4000 pixels. You would need an image that's 3200 x 4000 pixels (12.8 MP) to make a very good inkjet print.

If you had a file that was 2400 x 3000 pixels, that's equivalent to a 16 in x 20 in print at 150 ppi.

When ordering prints online, the company should be able to warn you when you reach the upper limit of print sizes so that you don't order a print that won't look good.

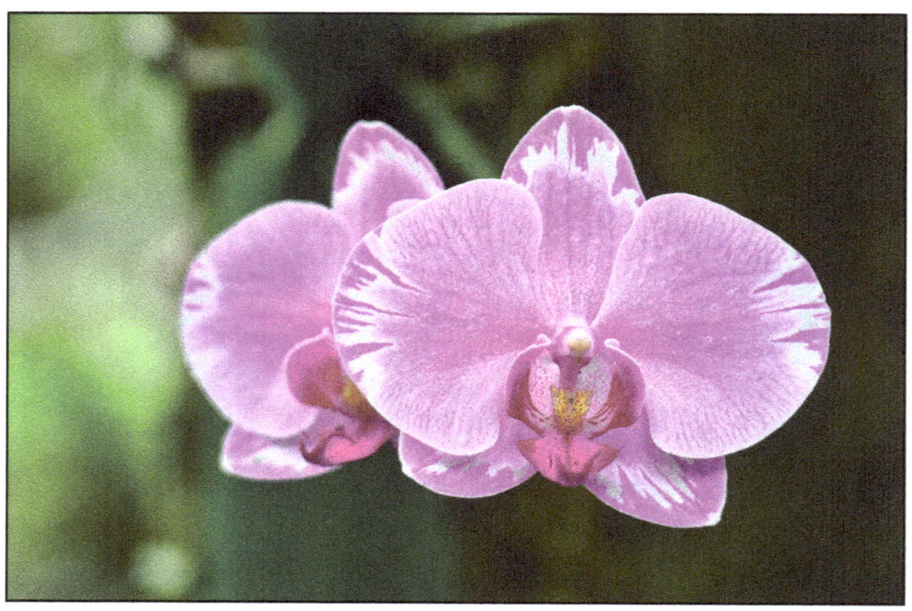

Orchid. Nikon D7000, manual, pattern metering, 1/6 sec, f/5.6, ISO 200, -0.3 EV, 120 mm. Hawaii Tropical Botanical Garden, Hawaii. The original digital file was 4928 x 3264 pixels. At 300 ppi, the print would be approximately 11 in x 16 in or 16 in x 24 in at 200 ppi.

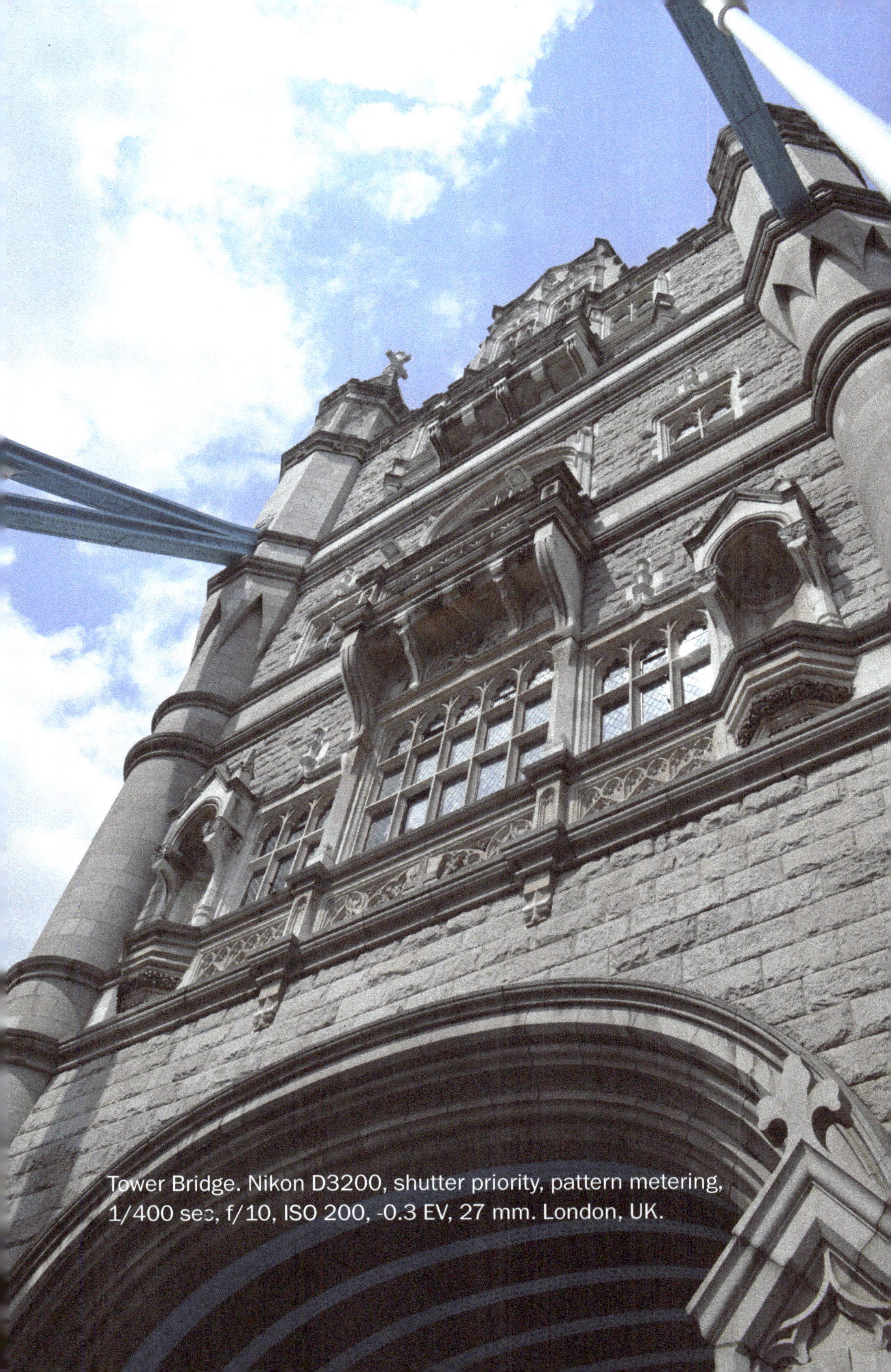
Tower Bridge. Nikon D3200, shutter priority, pattern metering,
1/400 sec, f/10, ISO 200, -0.3 EV, 27 mm. London, UK.

15.

Backing Up Images

Digital images, like any other file on your computer, should be backed up periodically. That is, make a copy of all your important images and save them to a thumb drive, external hard drive, and/or a cloud storage option.

As much as we'd like to think we'll get some kind of warning before our hard drive crashes, you really can't count on it. Get in the habit of saving your photos on a regular schedule (such as weekly, monthly, or even quarterly depending on how often you're adding new photos to your computer).

An ideal backup solution happens automatically and saves your precious images off site so that if something catastrophic happens to your home, you haven't lost all of your recorded memories in one fell swoop.

As digital cameras improve and you upgrade equipment, your photo files will increase in size so be sure your backup solution can handle the amount of storage you need now and well into the future.

16.
Inspiration

There are plenty of photographers past and present that can inspire you. Some of the more famous names include:

- Ansel Adams
- Margaret Bourke-White
- Jim Brandenburg
- Harry Callahan
- Anne Geddes
- Gary Hart
- Dorothea Lange
- Annie Liebovitz
- Sally Mann
- Steve McCurry
- David Muench
- Galen Rowell
- John Shaw
- W. Eugene Smith
- Alfred Steiglitz
- Art Wolfe

No list is exhaustive. There are probably photographers in your life that inspire you; and they don't have to be famous! Studying photographs that connect with you can help you improve your own photography. Explore Flickr, Instagram, and Pinterest.

Search on Google. Browse the photography and fine art section in the library or bookstore. Go to art shows, museums, and craft fairs to find photographers and other artists that are both similar and different from you.

As with any art form, practice is essential: continue to create, analyze, and create more. Attend workshops and classes to hone your skills and meet other photographers. It's not enough to know that a slower shutter speed will blur the action, you need to use different settings, under different conditions; see what worked and what didn't so you can try something new or be more confident the next time you are out with your camera.

17.

What Settings Do I Use?

Are you having difficulty figuring out where to start or what settings to change? Try these flow charts and troubleshooting tips.

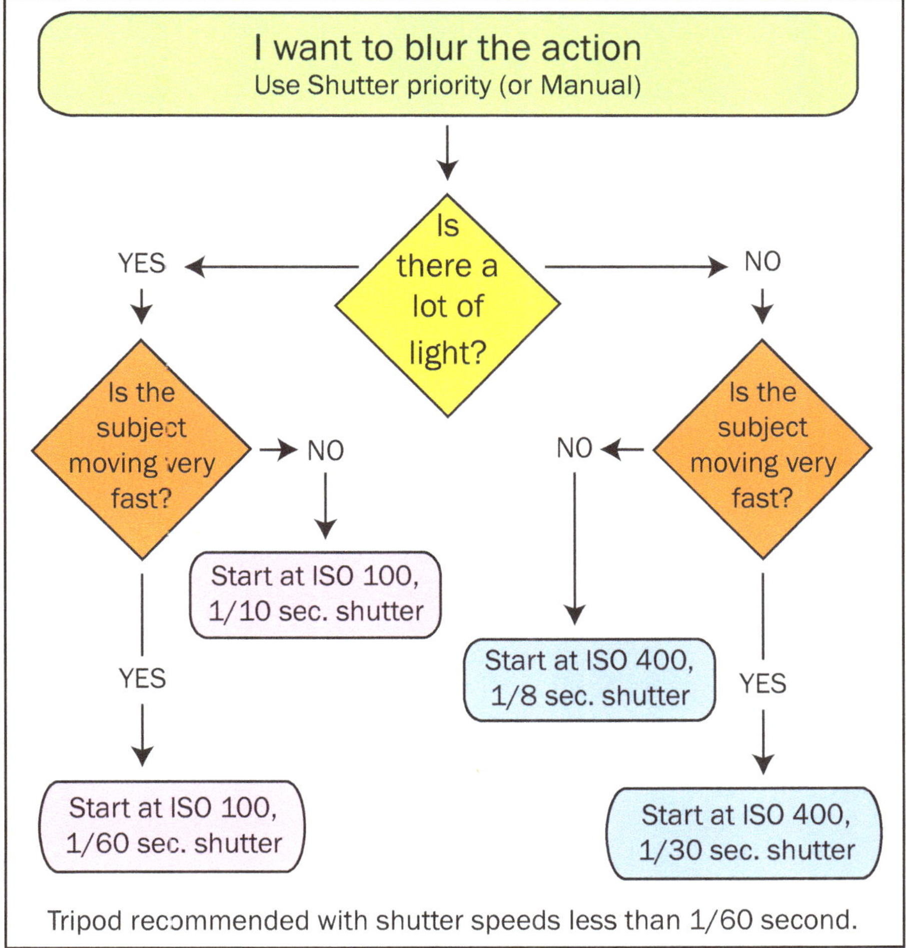

Table 16-1. Starter settings to blur the action.

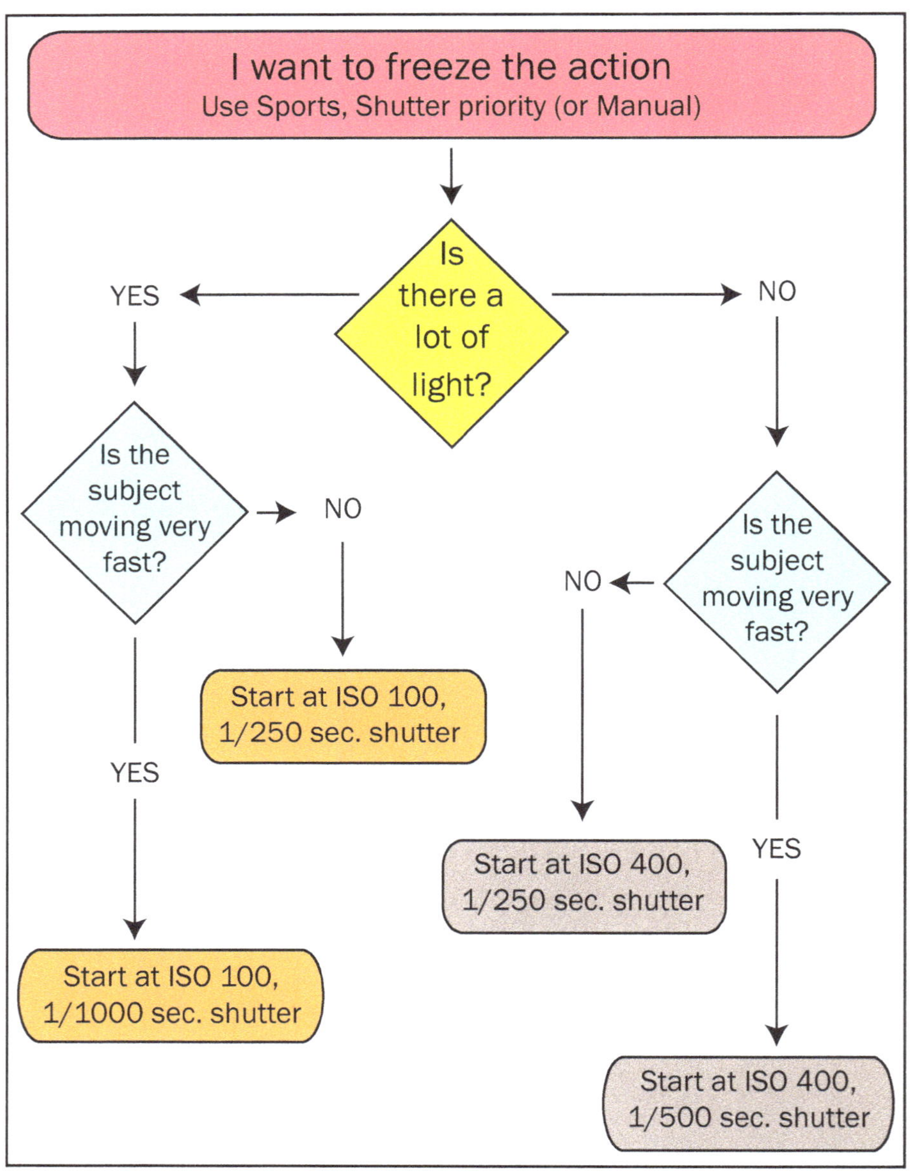

Table 16-2. Starter settings to freeze the action.

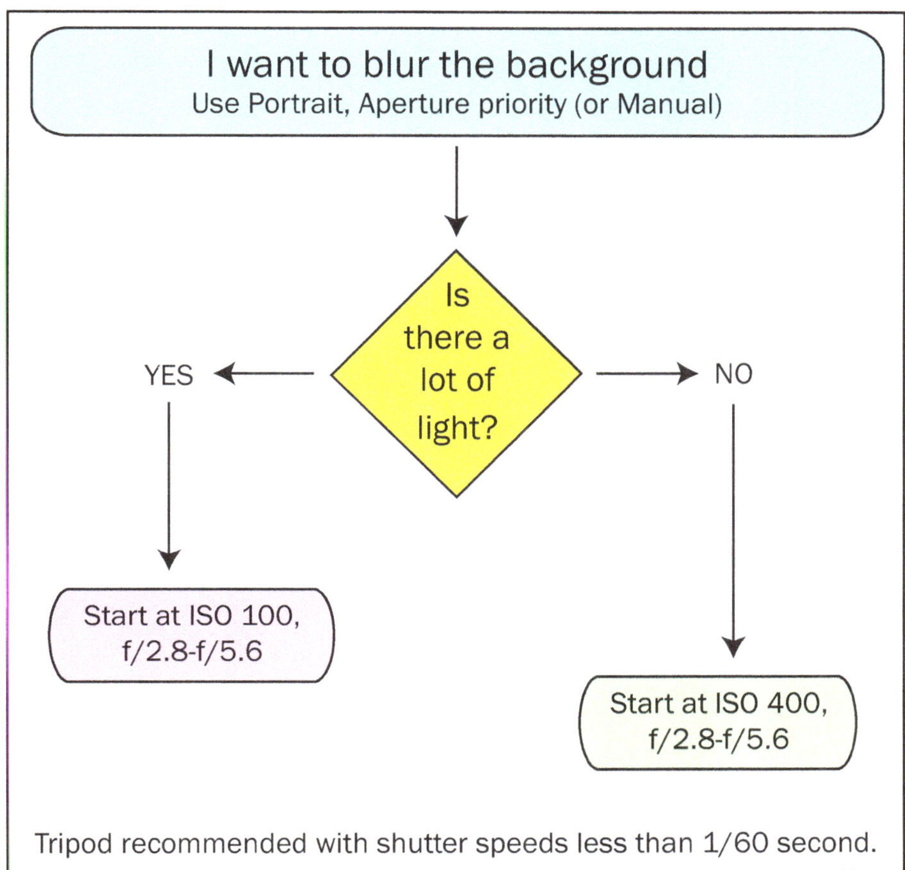

Table 16-3. Starter settings to blur the background.

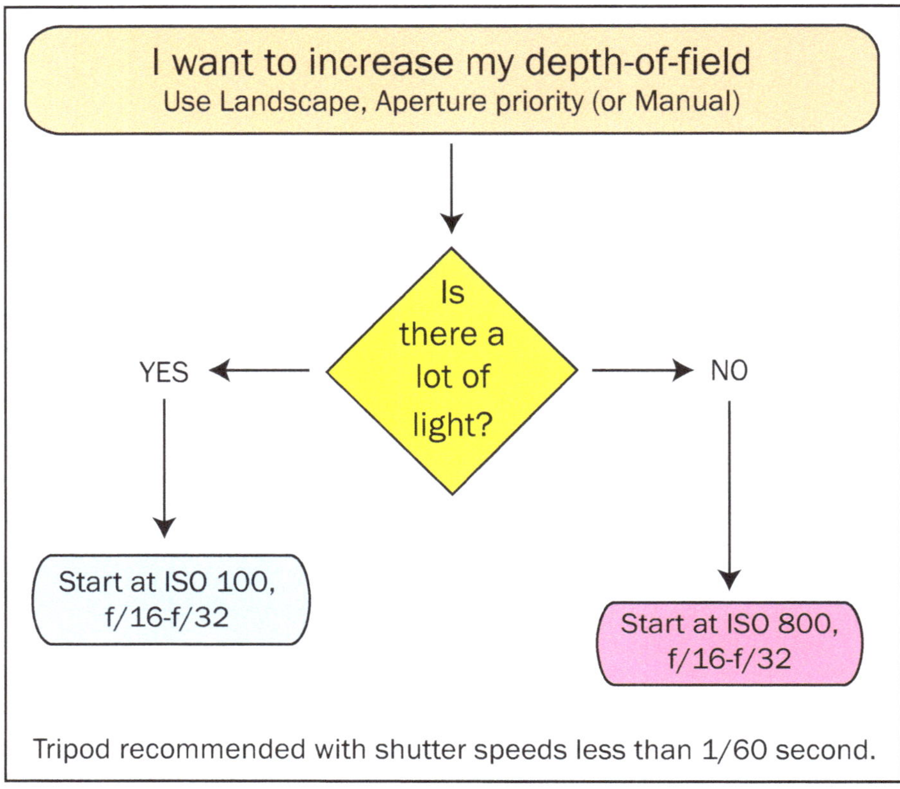

Table 16-4. Starter settings to increase your depth of field.

Bear in mind that these are suggestions of where to start with your settings. You may find that for a specific situation, you will wind up using settings that could vary greatly from these flowcharts. That's ok!

As you become more familiar with photography and how changing your shutter, aperture, and/or ISO affects the results, you will better anticipate what settings to use in each situation you encounter.

Troubleshooting

My photo is too dark. Add more light by slowing your shutter speed, widening your aperture, or increasing your ISO. You can also try exposure compensation (positive numbers) if it's just a little too dark.

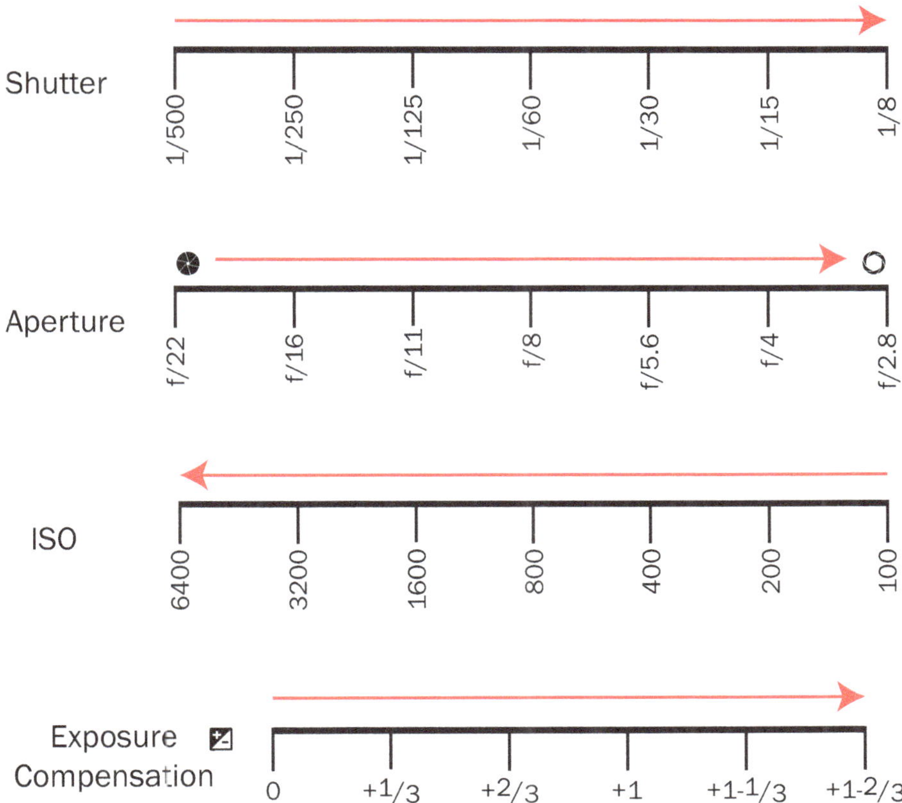

My photo is too bright. Reduce the amount of light by increasing your shutter speed, narrowing your aperture, or decreasing your ISO. Use exposure compensation (negative numbers) if you need to make a smaller adjustment.

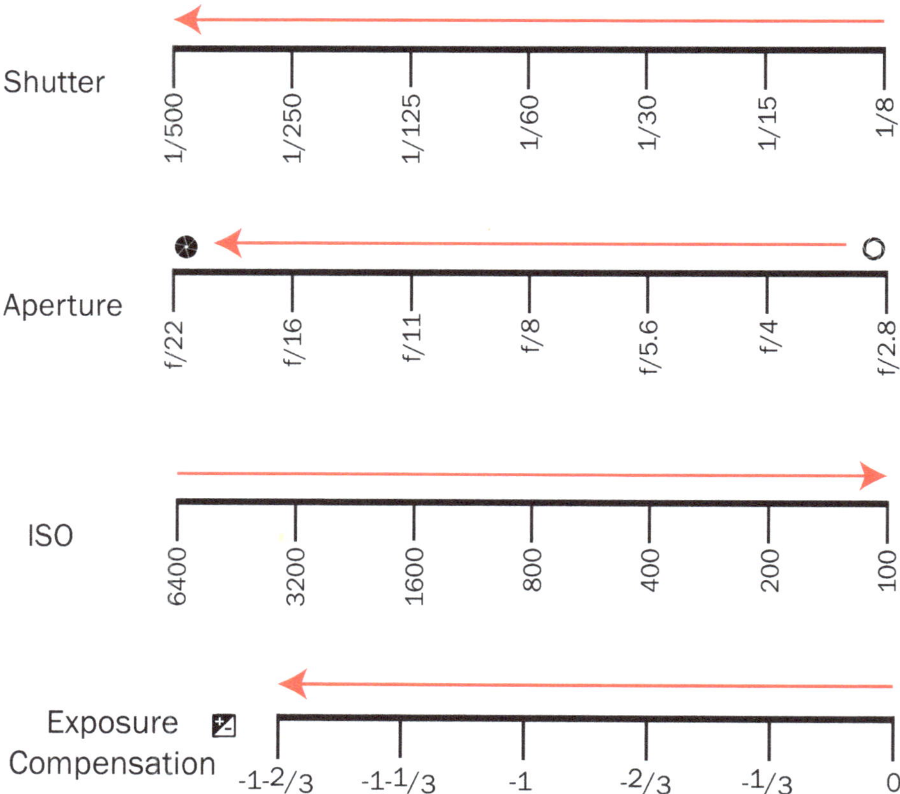
Shutter
1/500
1/250
1/125
1/60
1/30
1/15
1/8
Aperture
f/22
f/16
f/11
f/8
f/5.6
f/4
f/2.8
ISO
6400
3200
1600
800
400
200
100
Exposure
Compensation
-1-2/3
-1-1/3
-1
-2/3
-1/3
0

My subject is blurry. You need a faster shutter speed. Increase your ISO, if needed.

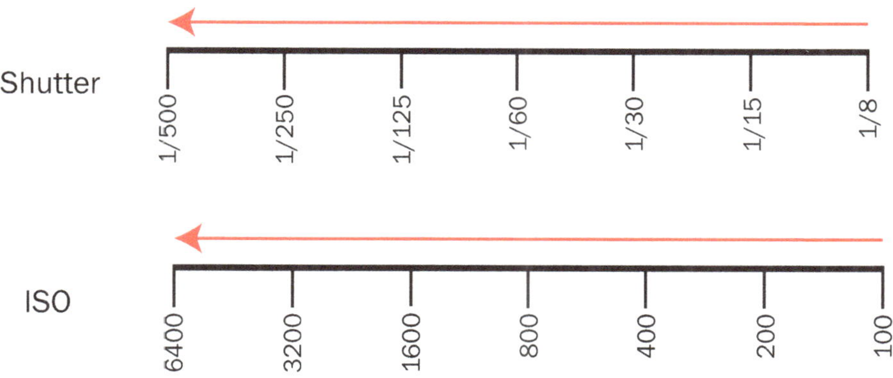

My subject isn't blurry enough. Use a slower shutter speed and perhaps lower the ISO. You may need a tripod to keep the rest of the image sharp.

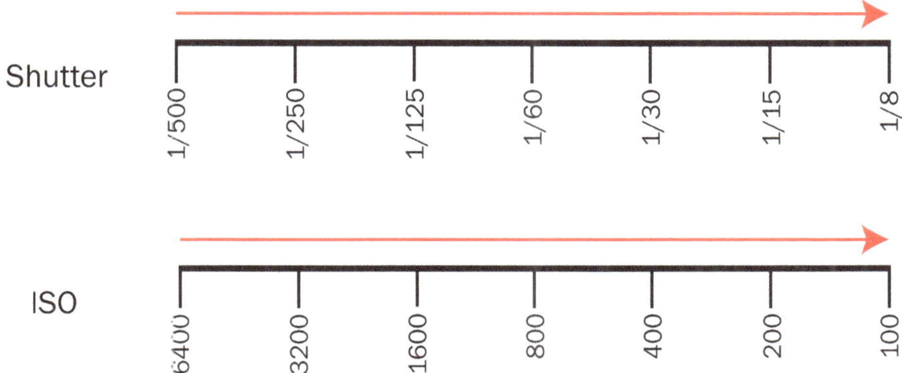

The background is too sharp. Try widening your aperture or using a telephoto lens.

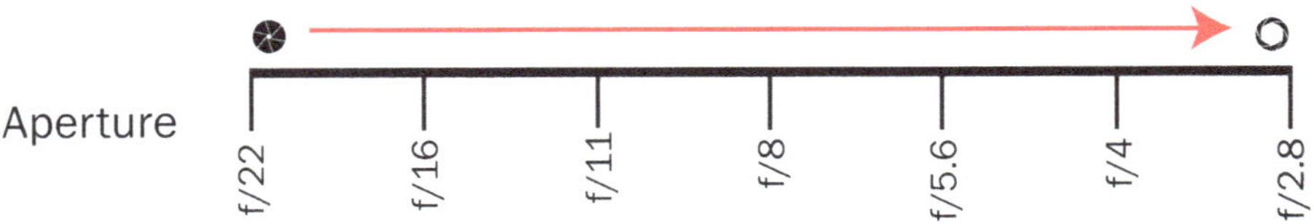

The background is too blurry. Use a smaller aperture or wide angle lens.

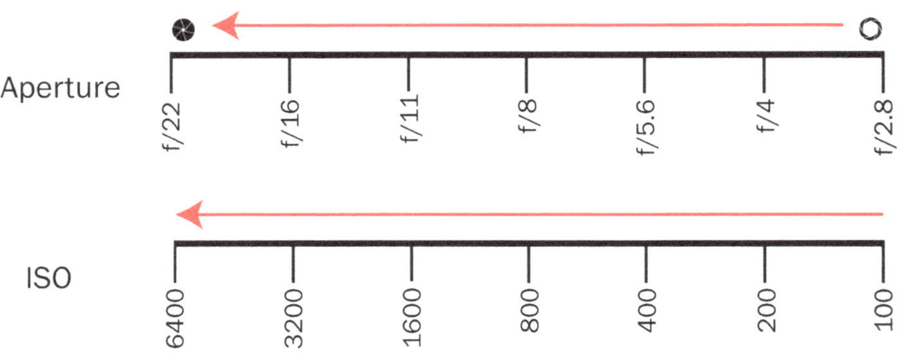

The color looks "funky." Your white balance needs adjusting.

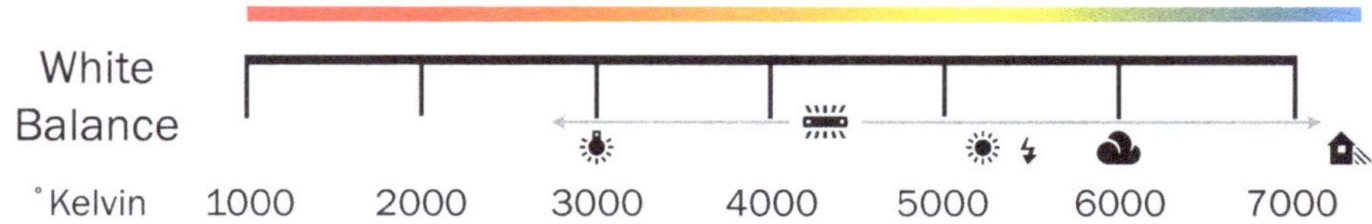

116

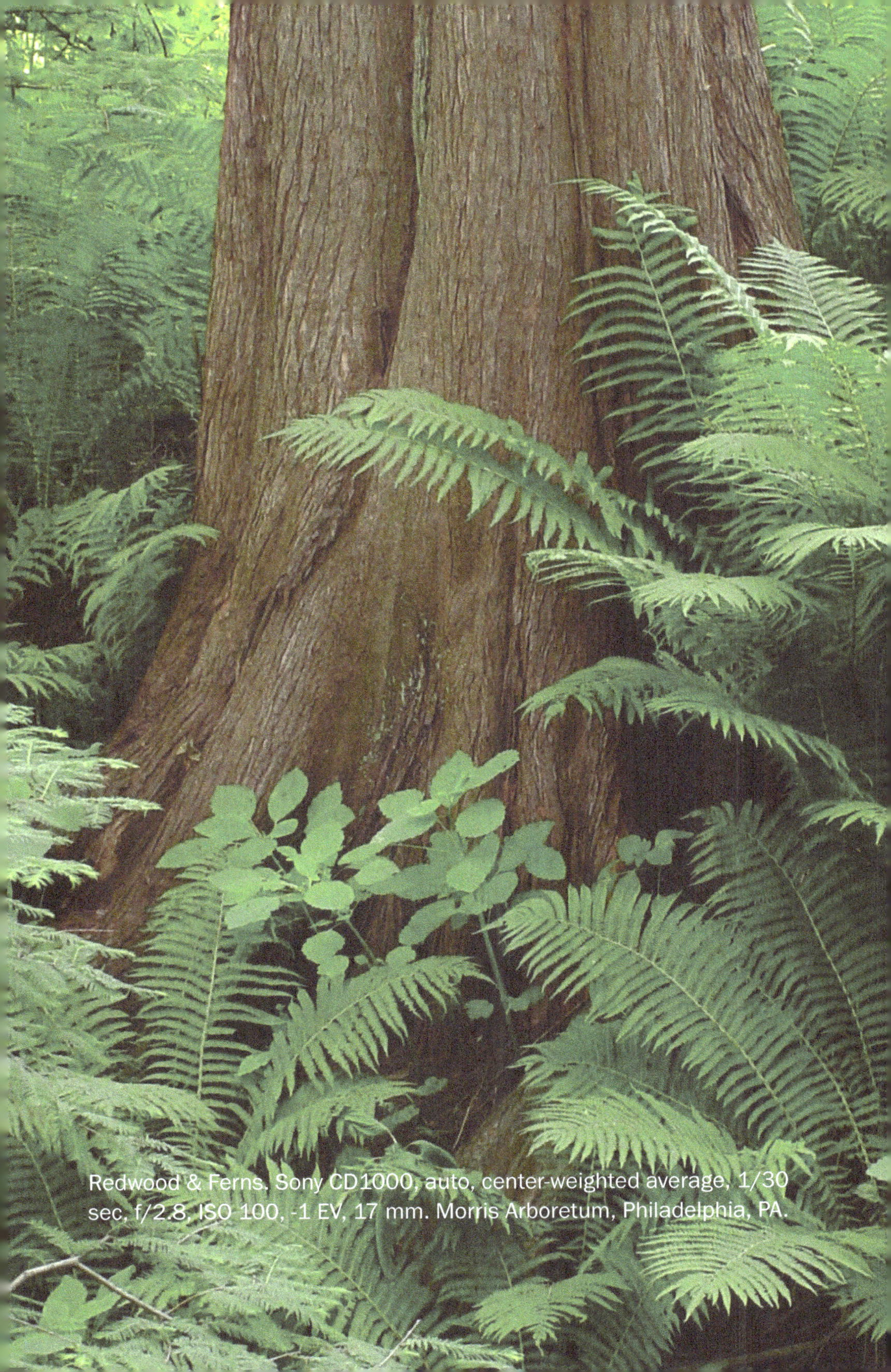

Redwood & Ferns. Sony CD1000, auto, center-weighted average, 1/30 sec, f/2.8, ISO 100, -1 EV, 17 mm. Morris Arboretum, Philadelphia, PA.

About the Author

My introduction to photography began in fifth grade when I received my first camera before a trip to Mexico. This little point-and-shoot had very few features, the negatives were tiny, and my pictures weren't very good. But I was hooked! I loved recording what I saw outside, whether at home or on family trips. My dad and grandfather encouraged me to just keep shooting.

My first digital camera in 2001 was a 2.1 MP Sony that recorded onto mini CDs. Technology continues to improve and cameras with 10 times the resolution (and more!) are readily available today. While the technology has changed, the knowledge necessary to make good images remains the same. Photography is about light and vision; and giving the viewer something to experience.

I started teaching others about digital photography in 2006. It's very rewarding to see my students discover the different results they can achieve with their cameras just by making a few adjustments.

You can visit me online at www.Toizer.com and on Facebook at ToizerPhotoDesign.